THE PROCESS

THE PROCESS

WHY LIFE HURTS
and
WHAT YOU CAN DO ABOUT IT

A PRACTICAL GUIDE
FOR UNDERSTANDING YOURSELF
AND
A WORKBOOK FOR CONSCIOUS
SELF-CREATION

by
Jeff Boyer
and
INNER WORK

THE PROCESS. Copyright © 2005 by Jeff Boyer and INNER WORK. All rights reserved. Printed in the United States of America. No part of this book may be used or reproduced without written permission from the author. For contact information: http://www.isbn4Authors.com
Cover illustration by Jim Best, Sacred Journey ceramics htt://hometown.aol.com/sacjour/myhomepage/index.html or sacjour@aol.com

ISBN 1-59971-047-1

Printed in the United States by Morris Publishing
3212 East Highway 30
Kearney, NE 68847
1-800-650-7888

TABLE OF CONTENTS

PART ONE
WHY? 1

PART TWO
PURPOSE 9
EXPLAINING THE PROCESS 10
A PROLOGUE TO PAIN 13
ABOUT PAIN 13
THE INFANT 15

PART THREE
STORIES 19
CHARACTER STRUCTURES 21
    SCHIZOID 21
    ORAL 22
    MASOCHIST 23
    NARCISSIST 24
    RIGID 24
THE DEVELOPING CHILD 25
MORE ABOUT STORIES 26
GOING DEEPER 27

PART FOUR
GETTING STUCK 33
THE ADOLESCENT 36
CHANGE 37
HELP 40
THE ROAD INWARD 41
RESISTANCE 42

DETERMINATION 45
PSYCHOLOGY/THEOLOGY 46
PSYCHOLOGICAL SUMMARY 47

PART FIVE
THE OTHER SIDE 53
SPIRITUAL REALITY 56
BACK TO THE BEGINNING 60

PART SIX
GETTING UNSTUCK FROM THE OTHER
    SIDE 65
TOOLS 66
TRUST 68
CHOOSING 70
MORE TOOLS 72
POSITIVE THINKING 75
GETTING PRACTICAL 77
GROUP ENERGY 80
THE LISTENING MODEL 81

PART SEVEN
GOING FORWARD 87
STAYING PRESENT 88
ALL ONE THING 89

WORKBOOK ....PAGE 92

POSTSCRIPT ....PAGE 109

PART ONE

THE PROCESS

THE PROCESS

WHY?

Why is life so uncomfortable at times? Why are relationships so difficult? Why don't other people understand us? Why don't they think the way we do, act the way we do? Why do people make us so angry? Why don't we feel the way others do? Why don't we know what will make those who are closest to us happy? Why do we often feel like we are frauds, pulling the wool over other peoples eyes? Why do we feel insufficient, incomplete, and powerless! These are some of the issues we will address in the coming pages.

Each person's life, and experience of it, is different, yet not so different. We all experience pain, and we all seek to be free from it. At the core, we all want to love and be loved unconditionally. We want to be accepted as we are. We want to trust and be trusted. We want to feel like we belong, really belong. We want to know that our life is meaningful, that it has purpose.

Life was never really meant to be painful, but it is far too often experienced that way. Everywhere we look we see manifestations of pain in this life. In my own life, I have seen that this experience can be changed, and that it is a choice. That is why I am writing this book. I must share what I have learned and assist as many people as I can. I feel compelled to offer the information I think is helpful for other people who are ready to make that choice as well. This is who I am and this is my purpose, for now. I have spent the last twenty five years actively searching for the cause of my own discomfort and attempting to alter that result. Part of the motivation to write this book came out of that search and the eclectic manner in which I chose to pursue it.

Dipping into many different psychological approaches from primal scream and psychoanalysis to new and currently developing techniques, I felt a piece of each to ring true, but none made total sense. The same was true of the spiritual aspects of my growth and understanding. I was raised in a traditional protestant church, but as the years went by I became disenchanted with the limited point of view and the rigid belief structures, not to mention the silent judgment. Most of the religious traditions I saw around me were intolerant of other spiritual paths. At the time, I thought that if there really was a God out there, that created everything, then it certainly would not choose one part of creation to be right and the other parts to be wrong. It seemed to me that the most important aspects of religion were those spiritual aspects shared by all. This led me to look into the realms of mysticism, where regardless of history and denomination, agreement centered around the limitless possibilities of experiencing the Divine in everyday life. I also felt called to study in the areas of hypnosis, channeling, different forms of energetic healing, and physical therapy.

The psychological studies gave me an understanding of peoples motivations and defense mechanisms. The energetic healing experiences led to a different kind of understanding of this physical existence, one that includes much more than can

THE PROCESS

be seen. I learned to feel the energy that is in, around, and through all living things. This has been a constant reminder of a greater reality for me. The study of trance channeling gave me a greater perspective on a transcendent reality beyond the everyday world. Meditations of all kinds led to a sense of awe about the power of the mind to produce or block feeling and the expansiveness that is possible when the mind is totally quieted. The physical training gave me a deep appreciation for the complexity of these bodies we live in and the miracle they represent. My experiences, as a whole, gave me an awareness of how what we choose to think and feel and do affects us and becomes manifested in all aspects of our lives, including our bodies. I could see how we literally create our lives and our experiences.

Still there were problems with this nest of learning I had gathered to me. It still felt fragmented. I was frustrated when trying to convey an experience or perception, or when trying to answer questions about what I believed. When trying to help a friend who was suffering, I could not figure out which frame of reference to work from. I began to realize that all these things I had delved into attempted to explain aspects of this life or its purpose, but the problem was they were all coming from different and limited perspectives. Each on its own left out too much to answer the essential questions of why life hurts and what we can do about it. I believe these are the essential questions because the pain we experience in life is either what motivates us to change or what blocks us from doing so.

I began looking at the similarities in these different philosophies and view points. There was some reason that I had selected these particular learning experiences and I was determined to figure out how they fit together. What I really wanted to know was how I fit into all of this. I wanted to understand how I could use what seemed to be outside normal experience to help myself and others to transcend the perceived boundaries of ordinary life. Trying to convey this kind of material is almost ridiculous because it attempts to explain the unexplainable and teach the unteachable. But, most of my life has been about trying to know the unknowable, even though I did not know it. So, why not give it a try!

    I have come to a place in my life where I realize that the only way to experience more happiness than I already have is by sharing it with others. That is what this book is about, sharing what I have learned about life, how it works, how we get stuck in the "Process", and how we get unstuck. Most of what is written here is an amalgam of every author I have ever read or listened to, mixed with my own thoughts. But, some of what I have learned and tried to convey here came from meditations where I gained information or understanding about things not through thought processes but actually from letting go of thinking and just receiving from whatever you call that source that is beyond our normal five senses. I like to think of it as receiving gifts.

THE PROCESS

JEFF BOYER

THE PROCESS

PART TWO

JEFF BOYER

THE PROCESS

PURPOSE

This book is an attempt to bring together aspects of psychology with mysticism and metaphysical spirituality in a way that will more fully answer the questions of *why* life hurts and what *you* can do about it. I hope that it helps you on your path to consciously creating the life experience you want. I have included, in the back, a workbook which will allow you to further investigate some of the ideas put forth here. It may also give you the opportunity to make some conscious choices and changes in your life, should you so desire. As you read through the book you will find markers indicating an item that is linked to an exercise in the back. You may choose to take a break from reading to investigate a particular exercise or save the workbook for later.

In order to even go into this subject about life as a "process" you need to first ask yourself the question, "is there a purpose to life"? If you think about it for a while I am sure most of you will agree that your life has purpose, you are just not sure what it is. Purpose and process denote the presence of some kind of plan and some greater story. As I will explain later, where you see yourself in relationship to this greater story, a bigger picture, directly affects your ability to change, and how different your experience of life can become. Everyone lives according to some larger story, but most never even think about the rules or guidelines that make up the bases of that story. They act based on unknown forces without wondering why! They are actors trapped in an unseen play, their drama, their story.

Story is the perfect place to begin this discussion. I say discussion because I would like you to think about, evaluate, and feel out the ideas in this book. Don't take my word for it. Try on what you find and see how it feels in your heart. Keep what works and leave the rest. But before getting started be sure to read the warning below.

WARNING: If you have not yet embarked on a conscious journey of self discovery, this is your last chance to turn away. Once you start down the path of self-awareness there is no turning back or turning it off. You will know that you are far more than your story and your pain!

EXPLAINING THE PROCESS

So what is this process that I am talking about? Let me explain by starting with what it is like before we consciously engage the process. Where we start is in a state of total unconsciousness, completely unaware of our true circumstances, we therefor have no control over our suffering. But, if our suffering becomes great enough, unbearable even, then we may seek to change it, and not continue the path of avoidance (dance around the void) that has yielded no real change or protection to this point.

THE PROCESS

So what is actually happening in this unconscious painful situation we call life? Two things are happening, one we can consider our psychology and the other our level of awareness. In our psychology, the stories of our wounding as children and the resulting compensations and coverups literally run our lives. We simply react to our perceived circumstances and feel we are doing the right thing, the only thing we can or should do. We are totally unaware of what really motivates us underneath the day to day stuff. What we don't know is that we are trying to avoid suffering, but attract it instead. We literally create the circumstances we are trying to get out of. The second part is our awareness level which is literally the ability to step back and watch ourselves in action and ask the questions who am I really and why do I feel the way I feel. As long as we are unable to see ourselves objectively, we remain unaware and literally are our emotions, and they toss us around like a tiny boat on an angry sea.

So the PROCESS is the **conscious investigation** into our story and what motivates us, as well as working towards **objective observation** of our feelings. This does not mean the cessation of feelings but rather *us having them, not them having us.*

So as we begin the process we investigate our story, find the wounds, find the defense mechanisms that were created to protect us from further suffering. These reactions no longer serve us but rather perpetuate the cycle of suffering. Within this arena we want to change two things, one is our patterned reactions which include our tendencies to blame ourselves or others, to run away, to stuff feelings down, or work harder to fix it all and make it right. The other change is to stop avoiding the feelings under the suffering, the painful feelings of our childhood wounds. Not everyone can do this right away and it may take years to get there. Fortunately our level of awareness can be worked on at the same time we are doing our psychological work. Raising one's level of awareness involves discipline and determination. It is a process of quieting the noisy mind to discover what is underneath in the silence of the void, the space between thoughts, between breaths. It is impossible to describe what the experience is like for it is different for each person. What I can tell you is that what you find there in the nothingness is the only thing that really lasts, the only thing that is really real. Everything else will eventually vanish, fade, die. The you that is found in the void is now and always will be. It is having this perspective or even approaching this perspective that takes the seriousness out of our perceived troubles and the suffering out of our pain. What used to be painful, even unbearable, becomes simply a temporary situation.

So in both the psychology and awareness arenas it is about objectivity. This is not an escape as some people might label it. I am not talking about viewing your life as a spectator in the audience. What I am suggesting is moving toward a state of being where you are the actor in a play, but you are also the playwright, the director, and the audience all at once. Enjoy the show!

THE PROCESS

A PROLOGUE TO PAIN

Once upon a time there was a child who knew that she was love. She was love and one with all the love in the universe. She was one with all that was, and floated in the ecstacy of the moment. Then she was born, and opened her little human eyes for the first time. She knew her mother just by the connection they had for the previous nine months, and still had at that moment. The child was laid on her mothers belly and they were one again, and yet one for the first time also, because this was different. Now the child was dependent on the mother's consciousness to provide for all of her needs. Before this, the mother's body had provided everything before any need was known. When the child needed something now, she had to cry out for she had no language and the mother failed to meet her needs before she herself was aware of them. Something had happened, something had gone wrong! They were no longer one, the way they used to be, they were also separate and the child became frightened. Until now she had always been safe and no thought about it had been needed. Now she had to concern herself with her own needs, and ego was born. And so began her pain.

ABOUT PAIN

If you are reading these words you know something about pain. Pain just seems to come with being human. Some of you may be intimate with this pain while others of you may keep the awareness of it at arms length. This pain manifests in many different forms. For some of you it is primarily in your relationships. You may feel inadequate and be afraid of the other leaving. You may be angry that the other is not living up to the expectations you had at the beginning of the relationship. Maybe the other does not seem to share their feelings with you, or they just won't listen when you feel the need to talk about your feelings. You are in relationship and yet still feel alone. You are frightened or even angry in your relationship with the person who is most important to you.

Others of you may find your pain focused more in the outer world. You have never really been happy with your work, there are always people that irritate you and put you down, or maybe people are always expecting too much from you. Maybe doing a job right is extremely important to you, but those around you don't have the same standards. Maybe it's just that the world never seems to go your way with people cutting you off in traffic, the car needs repairs, the kids are getting in trouble or just asking for time and energy you don't feel you have to give. Maybe you feel it is your responsibility to take care of everyone else's needs and wants. Or maybe it feels like demands come at you from all over, with never enough time and energy to do it all and still have some left for yourself.

Whatever form it takes, pain hurts, whether it comes as anger, frustration, loneliness, depression, or fear and anxiety. People often don't want to be who they think they are because it hurts. Just look around at how many people look up to those who appear to be happy. Actors and actresses, models, singers, musicians and sports celebrities capture the minds and desires of many. We wish we were them. We want to be where they are because we think that pain won't be. **Wrong!** You don't have to look too deep to see that most of these celebrities are not only normal people but many have what seems like more than their share of pain. Abuse, infidelity and divorce, drug use, gambling and sexual addictions are but a few of the manifestations of celebrity pain that we see. Still we persist in looking outside of ourselves for the answer, the cure for the pain we feel. We want to run away, fight off, or deny the pain but it just does not seem to be working.

THE INFANT

As days and weeks and months passed the child spent more and more time, energy and thought on trying to get his needs met. He found the moments of oneness in total satisfaction growing fewer and fewer. When mother did not come immediately upon his first cry he thought what is wrong? What have I done wrong? What is wrong with me? When mother came but was not in a loving space, he was sure is was his fault. He tried everything, sent every signal that had worked before, but sometimes his needs were not deciphered and he fell into despair. At other times his parents came to him with smiling faces and love in their hearts and the child knew he was ok. He was sure that this too was somehow his doing as well, for he experienced himself as the center of all things. He repeated those things he thought made his parents happy and loving, but their responses were inconsistent. They came to the child with their own problems and their own stories in tow.

JEFF BOYER

THE PROCESS

PART THREE

JEFF BOYER

THE PROCESS

STORIES

Stories, we all have one. Maybe you were the oldest, the youngest, a middle child, the motivated one driven by heavy parental expectations. Maybe you were abused. Maybe you were the one that could do nothing right. Nobody loved you, your mother beat you, you never fit in or felt like you belonged, you were a loner. Nothing seemed to go your way. Maybe, you were the princess, the prince, or the blessed one who could do no wrong. Maybe you were the under achiever or over achiever. Maybe you were the smoother, the fixer, the mediator, always cheerful and helpful. Maybe you just watched life go by from a distance, as if outside looking in.

The first question is how do we get our stories? Where do they come from? Do we inherit them? Are they given to us by our environment? Do we choose them? Or is it a combination of factors? Lets look at the psychology of it first. I will try to keep it brief and simple because it is not. Psychologists can drone on about this stuff for hundreds of pages until it becomes a thick ooze that you get bogged down in and never come out the other side with anything usable for the average person. Everyone's story is different, but there are some common themes. In psychology there are many different views and approaches to what I call stories. I cannot address them all nor would I want to. I will go into one that lends itself more readily to what I am trying to uncover in this book. In certain circles of psychology there are some things called character structures, which are a somewhat defined set of basic characteristics that we live with. These structures reside within our stories, and most of us came away from childhood carrying several of them.

A character structure describes the way we respond to life's challenges and how we prepare for its possible futures. Some say that they also describe body types, outstanding features, and postural abnormalities. Since pure character structures are really not seen and most of us are a mix, I won't go into those aspects because some people might feel locked into a structure by virtue of the physical attributes they have. It is more important to stay open to seeing how each of these structures may be working in you. You may have one dominant structure and the others play a minor role, or you may find that, as you unravel your story, they appear as layers, one getting worked through only to expose another acting itself out. I use them here as an acknowledgment of the work done in the field and because it is easier to use these already defined pieces rather than starting from scratch. In my experience, almost everyone who looks hard enough will find something in each story or structure that they can relate to.

THE PROCESS

CHARACTER STRUCTURES

There are five major character structures: Schizoid, Oral, Masochistic, Narcissistic and Rigid. Don't read anything into the names, they are just that names. And remember, cases of pure character structures are rare and most people end up with combinations to lesser or greater degrees. These structures develop in response to perceived trauma, in childhood. I will mention the age ranges where these were thought to occur but keep in mind that they can happen later as well. Let us just say that traumas occur and the way that we deal with them falls into these categories.

The following descriptions are a synthesis of the writings of Barbara Ann Brennan, Stephen M. Johnson and Carol Jud, as well my own thoughts, although the actual idea of these structures has been around for a long time. The descriptions here are not meant to be a full analysis of each one, but will give you a feeling for the different types of structures.

SCHIZOID

The Schizoid wound is a perceived hostile attack, threat, or abandonment by a parent or care-giver very early in life, conception to six months. The response is withdrawal into another world where it is safe, splitting off part of the self because it is too dangerous and painful to stay. Their major problems are feelings of fear and anxiety because to be fully present and feel is risking annihilation and death. This type needs love but fears abandonment, so "I'll reject you before you reject me" becomes the inner motto. They feel separate from the world and drift out of body at the first sign of danger. They tend to over-intellectualize, over-analyze and live in their heads. Underneath however, they may be enraged by the world that they believe wants to snuff out their life force. The message they received was "I have no right to exist". To feel better, they need to risk being alive and vulnerable, but the fear they face is that being alive equals certain death.

ORAL

The next structure, the Oral, suffers a perceived abandonment by the mother or care-giver usually around feeding, 6-18 months. Emotional or physical withholding occurred, giving but not enough, needs were repeatedly left unmet. Such a child eventually gives up trying to get their needs met. The child may become emotionally detached. They cling to the primary care-giver out of fear of further abandonment. But at the same time or soon after, they develop an early independence that seeks approval, seeks to please. The oral person feels empty and can never get enough. They complain of weakness and fatigue. They feel rejected by others and become both bitter about repeated rejection and fearful of asking for what they need. Unconsciously they are begging to be taken care of. Their cover up is "I won't need you, I won't ask". They need love, but feel that if they have to ask for it then it is not love, and if they don't ask for it, they will not get it. To feel better they must risk being abandoned by taking care of their own needs, but the fear they face is that taking care of me equals abandonment and death.

THE PROCESS

It is important to mention here a substructure of the Oral called the Symbiotic, which is in some ways an extreme of Oral. The symbiotic clings to their primary relationships as if their very life depends on it. Any threat to the relationship may cause extreme anxiety or a deepening depression to which they are prone. The symbiotic lives for the other because to think about what their own needs or wants are risks the unhappiness of the partner, the end of safety, and emotional death. Therefore any real strengths or aggressions are forbidden. This means the symbiotic has no self, in a way, and needs to risk surfacing their real feelings and not just the feelings that were created to assure continuance of their relationships.

MASOCHIST

Next we have the Masochist whose perceived wound is one of being "squashed", controlled and humiliated by the mother or primary care-giver, 18-36 months. In response, the child tries to hold in everything to avoid being humiliated. He or she becomes resentful and angered by the situation. Tension builds until finally, when provoked, they explode. Feelings of guilt and shame appear in response to their release or expressing of feelings and they turn in on themselves. They repeat a cycle of withholding and release and actually seek the provocation of others uncosciouslly so they will feel at least temporarily justified in their release. Their inner story says "I will kill myself before you do". Their major complaint is tension, and their problem is their inability to accept their own feelings. To feel better they need to risk expressing themselves, becoming vulnerable, but to do so means risking humiliation and death.

NARCISSIST

The Narcissistic wound is a perceived betrayal by the parent of the opposite sex in early childhood. The parent wanted something from the child and manipulated him or her. The love the child received was based on what he or she did, it was always conditional. As a defense, the child compensates by learning to manipulate and control the parent in return. Their fear is of being controlled or betrayed so they must always be the one in control, all the time. They will bully, undermine, or seduce to gain the power and control they seek. They feel they must be right or die, but rarely if ever feel really safe. Their major problem is feeling defeated. Deep down they would like to surrender and be supported, but to trust equals betrayal and death.

RIGID

The Rigid like the Narcissist experiences betrayal by the parent of the opposite sex but reacts by denying and withholding all feelings, usually between 5-12 years. If he or she admitted to having a complaint it would be not having any feelings. But, they will not seek this kind of help because they are most likely unaware and their need for control is too great. This type suffers from excessive perfectionism and competitive aggression. Deep down there is a desire to lower the walls and really be with another person but to allow feelings means certain rejection and death. There are variations of the rigid: the hysterical female, the masculine aggressive female, the passive male, and the phallic narcissistic male. I don't need to go into these, and in fact in some psychological circles, the Rigid is believed to be just a variation or extreme of the Narcissist.**(Ex#1)**

THE DEVELOPING CHILD

So the child went through her first few years surviving the painful adjustment from total peace without awareness of needs, to one where needs often went unmet. Some of these needs were as simple as knowing she was loved unconditionally. Her parent's energy and behavior did not always support this knowing and so she could not trust in it. Occasionally, her parents even got angry when she cried and tried to make her stop. They tried to force her to lay down alone and go to sleep when she wanted to be held and loved and reassured. This was a frightening response coming from her only source of care and safety. Her waking hours became focused on trying to feel out ways to get her needs met, and how to make her parents happy instead of angry. Since she was the center of the universe, she was responsible for her experiences of happiness and pain. The presence of pain and her parent's inconsistency was evidence that there was something wrong with her. She was defective in some way and therefore not only accepted the pain as a reality but also began to expect it. The continued presence of pain confirmed her belief that she was no good.

MORE ABOUT STORIES

Ok, we got through that part. Whew! I hope I didn't lose too many on the way because it's not as bleak as it sounds. Positive qualities tend to emerge from these stories as well and later in the book we will go into some possible reasons for that. It also takes a variety of personalities to make the world interesting and worth being in. If everybody was the same it would be way too boring. What would be the point if we were all exactly the same? Here are some of the pluses: Because of his or her wounds and the resulting compensations, the Schizoid often develops a keen intellect or a deep sense of spirituality. The Oral develops wisdom and serenity. The Masochist develops a large heart and the ability to nurture. The Narcissist develops courage, integrity and leadership, and the Rigid a sense of order and harmony. Here we can start to see the "process" where we are born into situations that wound us, wounds that we must deal with in some way or another as we try to find a way to compensate for our pain and find at least some happiness, a sense of safety, and an outlet for expression of inner feelings and drives. This endeavor results in the development of gifts to a greater or lesser extent that add to the texture of this life we all live. This also forms a basis for a large part of what we call our personality, which we will be discussing later. **(ex#2)**

THE PROCESS
GOING DEEPER

Ok, ok let's get to the part about why life hurts and what we can do about it, right? Because its not actually the story that hurts. If you remember I was careful to say perceived wounds in relation to the character structure's stories because there can be a great variance in the actual insult to the child, as well as the reaction from the child. I am not saying that a child who was raped did not actually experience the act, but rather that different children experience the same type of situation differently. One may have been the recipient of a literal abandonment, and yet respond as if it was not life shattering, while another child who's mother was separated for only a short time after birth might split off into another realm because to stay was too traumatic. So in the end, it isn't actually what happened that is important, but rather what the child did with it. The pain was not in the act itself. The pain was in the child's inability to allow the experience of the feeling response. In order to save the self from certain annihilation, the child had to do something else with the feeling. The choices were to split off part of the self and leave, give up the self and its needs and take on trying to please the parent, withhold any outward expression and try to push the feelings down, take charge dominating through coercion or seduction, or lastly refusing to feel and denying the need to. Of course these choices are made at different stages, and so several can be, and are, adopted and exist within the same individual.

So, are you starting to see yourself in here somewhere? Do you drift off into daydreams when things get tough, or over intellectualize as a way of not feeling things? Are you often fearful, or tense, a shallow breather? Do you sometimes feel like you don't really have a right to live, that others are more important than you? Do you attempt to overcome these feelings by trying to be intellectually or spiritually special? This is the Schizoid story!

Does your life seem to revolve around trying to make sure that everyone is happy? Are you an anger rejecter, denying your own anger and fearful of another's? Are your intimate relationships so important that you will do anything to not upset the applecart even when you feel your needs are not getting met? Do you have sex as a way to get the closeness you need? Do you feel empty and hollow, desiring to be filled, but have no idea what you really need? Have you learned to get some of your needs met by giving and nurturing others, but occasionally succumb to depression? This is the story of the Oral or Symbiotic!

Do you feel tense, trapped, defeated, or humiliated, with a pervasive sense of guilt and shame? Are you polite but a little bit whiney and negative in order to get people to agree with what you want or do you hold in your feelings about things until someone makes you mad, then explode and later feel bad about it. Do you get the attention and recognition you need by doing things for others, by self sacrifice and at the same time resent it? Do you feel like your mother has power over you? Do you feel like you have to hide your feelings or others might use them against you? This is the Masochistic story!

Does it seem like the world is plotting against you, other people are always doing things to you or making things

THE PROCESS

difficult for you? Do you find yourself frequently getting upset because other people are not doing the right thing or doing it the right way? Are you driven to succeed in business and organizations and groups, but not really able to enjoy the fruits of your labor? Do you feel like no matter how well you do, it isn't good enough, that you could and should do more? This is the Narcissistic story!

Is your primary problem in life the failure to have successful, fulfilling relationships? Are you attracted to potential partners either sexually or in a loving way but not both? Are you attracted to people who are unavailable but lose interest when they become available? Do you worry about your lack of feelings, or are you confronted by your partner about being emotionally unavailable? Do you find yourself needing to be right no matter what? This is the Rigid story!

JEFF BOYER

PART FOUR

JEFF BOYER

THE PROCESS

GETTING STUCK

So again, the question is "why does life hurt?" Life hurts because we got stuck! We *all* got stuck. We got stuck because we were unable to allow the feelings associated with the original painful experience. Sensing that it was the same as death we turned it off, cut it off, projected it outwards, or denied its existence. We did not want to feel that way again, and so we developed ways of protecting ourselves, or at least tried to. More importantly, we began to see the world through the filter of that experience. We live with the fear of more experiences like it and the intolerable feelings they bring. Our personality, our "I", is to a great extent, a collection of reactions to events and their perceived positive or negative effects on us. We defend, deflect, or try to prevent the pain from coming back, and yet cling to the pain of those early insults.

We often don't have direct access to the original event that we "got stuck in", but continue to live with the feeling it produced, in reaction to current events. These are sometimes easy to see when we "make mountains out of mole hills" and our reactions are disproportionate to the situation at hand. We may totally lose it over something minor like when a child does not listen to something we said or just for making too much noise. We may present with irrational fears of groups or authority figures, of showing our feelings in front of strangers or showing them in public at all. We may have a panic attack when we are having an argument with someone we care about and they suddenly walk out. We may contract in fear when someone in the room gets angry, maybe even feel like we are going to get sick. We might feel worthless or depressed when someone we love is in pain, and there is nothing we can do about it. We may know that we are overweight but feel starved all the time. Maybe we can't eat at all when we get nervous, or it actually becomes difficult to breathe. Maybe we go from job to job , but it always feels like people are against us or we can't respect them and eventually quit. We may even, in time, come to realize that a different way of being or doing things would have a beneficial effect on our lives, but we have difficulty making the change or making it stick. We want to change and we tell ourselves we should, but still can't. We go through our daily lives trying to avoid pain. In other words, we are afraid. **(ex#3)**

That is actually the funny part, or not so funny. We act as if we are in pain but in reality it is fear, fear of the pain. We are afraid of the pain that we are sure is coming soon. Now this may not sound like a healthy way to live, and you are right, but most people live their lives in fear, consciously or unconsciously. Now if this were the only thing keeping us from being happier, you could see how over time and with maturity the sting of the initial pain would fade, and we could move toward a less fearful state of being. But, it is worse than that. I can hear some of you now saying "how can it get worse than living in fear?" But it is true, we are not only stuck in our fear of pain, we are also stuck in identifying ourselves with our past pain, the original pain. The personality, the "I", has to some degree developed as a response to these painful situations and the idea of changing that threatens its very

THE PROCESS

existence. In fact, the ego/personality actually seeks out situations and experiences that will create similar pain, or at least trigger the same response. This behavior is an attempt to substantiate the chosen picture of life and of the self. The ego will choose pain over pleasure every time, because that validates its existence and its perceived picture of the world as a painful place.

The mind has created a picture of the "self" based on isolated memories. Why we choose the particular memories that we do is hard to say. Maybe there was a purpose and we can talk about that later, but right now picture this: you created a story based on isolated memories, some real and some made up, because memory is actually malleable. Your story is not the whole story, just a projection based on certain selected pieces. Did you paint yourself as a victim, a pawn, a hero, a villain, or a detached bystander? Regardless of what identity you created, your mind, and your ego/personality, are not going to give it up easily. The inner feeling is that "this is it, this is who I am and if I lose that there is nothing." "I will not exist." In most cases, we choose our memories, the pictures and images of our past based on the degree of impact they had on us and often that involved pain. Still we are not willing to give it up. Or *are* we? Pain is not only the curse, but also the blessing for without it we would have no motivating factors to help us change. It is only when people become intolerably uncomfortable that they are willing and motivated enough to risk change. **(ex#4)**

JEFF BOYER

THE ADOLESCENT

In adolescents there is a change with the rise of hormones that many see as chaos and turmoil. This is actually the time when the story has been solidified within the child, and at the same time, a new drive to override that story arises. Built into the physical human being is a second chance, a biological wake up call. Not only do they feel a desire to fight against the inner feeling world they find themselves in, they are compelled to. It is like they are being called to break out of the shell they have built around them and move toward some unknown purpose. In western society we see it as acting out and label it as bad. When this acting out is taken to extremes and unchecked, it may result in prison or worse. In other parts of the world, as Robert Bly speaks about in his book **_Iron John,_** this behavior is seen as a call for initiation into adulthood. This is when the mature older adults come into the picture and teach the young adult how to channel these *natural* energies. They undergo ritual and experience acceptance as a valuable and purposeful adult member of their tribe. Without this adult acceptance and guidance, we lash out at the world, try to run away, or feel we need to find ourselves somewhere else, anywhere other than here. The here that is meant is the feeling state they find themselves in. Suicide, reckless and anti-social behaviors abound until they break free of the old sense of self, or succumb to it. This is where our process of change either speeds up or slows down.

THE PROCESS

CHANGE

How do we go about changing what we have become, or more accurately, what we have created ourselves to be? To change the way you see yourself may require that you feel the feelings that were too much for the infant or very young child to tolerate. It may mean risking the expression of feelings that have been covered over and locked away long, long ago. This can open a space for the experience of being something different. It becomes an acknowledgment of the possibility of being more. At the same time it necessitates letting go of a part of how you see yourself now. This is a type of death and is experienced as such by the ego who's job it is to protect, hide and defend the perceived self, the inner child. I have heard people say why would I want to dredge up that old stuff. Why would I put myself through that? I can't even remember most of my early childhood and I am happy with it that way. My answer is, you wouldn't, not if you are truly happy with your life the way it is, and truly happy with you! As I said before it takes a variety of people to make this world work. Some people come through horrible childhoods and find a compensation that works. As long as it is working for you that is where you need to be. I don't believe in pushing people forward in their "process" because they become off balance, confused and in the end resentful. This introspective type of growth work is not for everyone. The journey toward awareness is one of free-will and needs to be consciously chosen, not forced. If you know there is something more out there and you feel the need to know, the call to find it and become it, then it is worth looking *inside*. That is where all the answers are regardless of how empty it may feel or how scary the idea may be.

Getting back to the theme of change, even when one wants to there will often be intense internal resistance and fear. Here I am talking about fear with a capital F. Many times I have seen people in the therapeutic process clinging to some elusive sense of self. They may literally be contracted on the floor like a tight fist. When they finally let go they experience a more expansive, lighter sense of being. You can actually watch them melt. It is as if some weight has been lifted, some curtain parted, some container opened. They come to find that they were clinging to nothing. It was an illusion. There was nothing there to hold on to, only an idea, an unconscious thought of fear just below the surface. What they find is that they were afraid of becoming something different, even though that is what they consciously want to do. The fear was of losing some identity, of death of some part of the self. This imminent change was expected to be painful and the ego wanted to run. There was a simultaneous ***desire*** and ***fear*** of feeling something different. This is when the knowledge of how stuck we can get becomes glaringly obvious.

This fear that most of us live with is tremendously restrictive and heavy. It takes most of our energy just to maintain the image, the way things are, the way things feel, as chosen by our wounded inner child. When it is released, let go of, then we are free to expand and grow. Then we open the door for something greater to enter and move through us resulting in a greater availability of energy. This is our life energy and even if the opening is only for a moment, there is an irreversible change that occurs. You are then no longer the same person, but one who has begun making conscious choices rather than living unconsciously. Even if it feels like you have fallen back into the depths of the old drama, ***you***

THE PROCESS

have not. Something else exists in you and you know it. No matter how bad things get you won't quite buy the whole thing, the whole story, as before. You have gained a bit of distance from the story because you know the story can change.

So the question is how do we change? How do we let go of what has been our truth, in order to find our new, our next in a series of truths? How do we let go of who we think we are so we can become who we could be or who we are meant to be? First, know your story, work with a counselor or an objective friend that you trust and look up to. Begin writing it down. There are exercises in the workbook that follows, designed to help with this process. Start by writing and discussing your earliest memories and what you have heard from family members and family friends. Fill in the blanks with what feels right or just make it up. Look for the places in the story where you would expect the main character (you) to get angry, frightened, or sad. Can you put yourself there and feel what you would expect someone to feel in that story. If so then that can be a doorway in for you. If not, you can with help, try the feelings on, imagine you are there in the story as it is happening. Be the child. See what happens. Some people can do this work on their own. They just let the feelings rise up in their bodies and play out the scenarios to their natural conclusions. This necessitates playing all the parts, or at least feeling all the parts including your adult self as mediator and protector of the child. It also takes an underlying belief or knowing that it is safe and will all work out in the end. If it does not feel safe to you then don't try it alone. Most find it easier to enlist the aid of a professional who works in this area. **(ex#5)**

HELP

Find someone trained in Core-Energetics, Bioenergetics, Body-centered Psychotherapy, Process Therapy, or some other mental health worker who is willing to work with the body, as well as the mind, and is not going to be ruffled by loud noise. These places where we get stuck are well defended. And when the door is opened and the repressed feelings are allowed to express themselves, things can get really hot on the way to the other side. Much is locked in the body because the feelings were too scary to keep in consciousness. It was safer to hide those feelings and experiences in the body. Sometimes working with the story gets the body involved, and other times, working with the body causes the feeling memory to return. Breathing deeply and moving the body around are essential because we react to fear by pulling in, tightening up, and stopping the breath. Breath equals life which for some can be too dangerous. Another powerful way to do this work is in groups. There you get the support of other people doing their own work. You also get lots of chances to get triggered by someone else's story. When you see and hear someone else dealing with an issue that you have buried deep inside you, the light may suddenly go on. Then you find the feelings welling up, and the story begins to reveal itself to you. A group setting also provides built in witnesses that help the experience seem more real, when the ego later tries to deny that it ever happened.

THE PROCESS

THE ROAD INWARD

So what we are talking about here is traveling back into childhood to revisit the wounding experience or experiences. So how does going back into that space where we got stuck help us? It helps because it gives us a chance to make a different choice. We cannot directly change the past but we can change its effects on us. When the adult *you* stands with the child *you* and shouts "NO", "THAT'S NOT OK", from a feeling state, something shifts. It shifts because for the first time the child perceives a different way of feeling, a different way of being, and a different way of reacting, one not based in fear. But it can only be done in the face of the feeling of the original fear, the one that formed all the defensive reactions that followed. Often this means working with a current situation that brings up the intense feeling reaction, and working through it to reveal the deeper layers. This may eventually reveal the original wound to be worked. If not, working with the new freed up energy and change in conscious reactions may be enough.

In some situations this involves letting the rage out that has been locked away in fear of being rejected, or the fear that it might kill. Other situations involve a letting go into an acknowledgment of pain, which after being embraced, gives way to anger or deeper into the fear itself. It is in acknowledging this deep fear, embracing the full feeling of it in the body and the emotions, and then making a different response to it that allows our energy to shift focus. We shift from a focus on death, and fear of it, to a focus on life, and an acceptance of its wonderful possibilities. There is a release, if only temporary, from a focus on the past and the future, and the perceived pain that dwells there. Instead you find yourself in the present moment, freely floating in the space of your own creative nature. In this space one can begin to reconstruct oneself in a new image, one that feels different, acts different, and reacts different. Life is permanently changed when you allow this kind of experience. By allowing the feelings to surface and embracing them as okay, including the child's initial response, the only one that was possible at the time, we are finally able to release it. We can stop clinging to the past. ***But***, there is resistance.

RESISTANCE

The first time is especially fraught with doubts. The personality goes to work trying to convince you that it never happened or that it was not real. The excitement of the change passes and if we don't stay vigilant, the old ways of feeling creep back in, even though we don't totally buy it anymore. If we don't keep the memory of the release and the pain free space that was created, we are likely to fall back into old patterns and therefor the old beliefs about ourselves. Remember, if given the chance, the ego/personality will always choose pain over freedom. In addition to our internal struggle regarding the experience's legitimacy, the world around us will also try to put us back in our old box. People don't particularly like it when we change unless they are in on it from the beginning. Those around you want you to stay the same so they can feel safe. They think they know who you are, and who they are in relation to you. But, if you start changing, that upsets the whole system. It means that they might be able to or even have to change, which is scary. They

THE PROCESS

might even feel that you expect them to change in order to continue the relationship. This threatens their fearful little child because it was not their choice. Your change just happened to them. Now, in order to substantiate their view of the world and make themselves feel safe again, they must trash your new experience and the appearance of any real change. They must return you to the box of your previous self. They will employ every unconscious trick in the book to get you to act and react the way you did before. They will attack, blame, coerce, seduce, plead, get panicked, sick, or leave. What ever worked in the past to make you angry, fearful or pained will be tried.

The basis for this reaction, as I have mentioned before, is "Fear". They are afraid of losing something. They may be afraid of losing the relationship and end up abandoned. Maybe it's just the specific role they played that they fear losing, for if that happens they no longer get the continual feedback that the ego/personality needs to substantiate the image of self. There are countless scenarios that exist between individuals which are carefully balanced to maintain the status quo of feeling how we do about ourselves. When you change, it affects the way the other sees him or herself. Whatever it is, they blame it on you in some way and try to get you back into the old box. It is important to remember that it is not your fault and *nobody* is to blame. All you are doing is seeking to be whole, to remember and release who you really are, without all the layers of illusion put in place by the ego. If we can remain centered in the new experience of expansiveness in spite of what is going on around us, we are in the "now." In the "now", we are not clinging to the past, focused on fear of the future, or dreaming of a future without pain. We can finally experience life in its unadulterated form, no expectations, only pure experience. We can experience what "is" and find that it is *all* "okay." Even when it hurts! In this place, truth becomes natural and either heals the rifts in our relationships as a result or facilitates their appropriate ending. If a relationship is based on lying or withholding it will have to change or end in order for you to maintain your new found sense of self and continue to grow further. Growth is not a one time experience, it is an ongoing ***process***. Those who shift once and exclaim "This is it....I have made it" delude themselves and simply cling to this slightly altered self, just as they did the previous one. It is like swapping one addiction for an other. Much of the original pathology remains, and the transforming experience is now used to further resist change rather than opening to it.

THE PROCESS

DETERMINATION

I know I am going on about this, but here is where you make it or break it. You make the choice to risk change, to get unstuck, and then are confronted with the consequences of that choice, the reactions to that choice, the resistance to change. Do you trust your inner self that led you to move forward in the first place and risk change, or do you succumb to the pressures, both internal and external, and collapse back into your old sense of self that does not really fit you anymore? Most people who risk this sort of change fall back several, or even many times, then rise and get back on track. Eventually, if you are to move ahead more steadily and more easily, you will start taking your cues from the *inner* you that knows what you need, what is best for you in the long run. Some people call it intuition; others call it inner guidance. You will often recognize it when you know a choice is best for your health, be it physical, mental or spiritual. You know it, but it is not the choice your ego/personality or inner wounded child wants. There is an inner conflict, two voices. One voice belongs to the ego/personality, the inner wounded child. The other voice is a deeper part of a more essential you. Be determined to keep listening, to stay focused on making conscious choices based on this deeper knowing, this deeper voice. This is where the spiritual aspects of the process start showing up.

PSYCHOLOGY/THEOLOGY

What I have seen with most people, is that if they stay with the work, this process, the psychological questions make way for the spiritual questions. "What is my relationship with God?" "Do I believe in God?" They move through feelings like "I am angry with God," or "How could God have done that to me?" To a large degree, these are the attempts of the wounded inner child to make some sense out of what can not be understood in ordinary ways. God can not be understood through the mind alone, and so it is useless to try and address these issues purely from a psychological point of view. At one level it is about the child trying to deal with a projected image of the Divine based on its own experience. To the child, God is a parental figure like his or her parents, full of contradictions. This God is angry, judgmental, jealous, as well as loving, kind, and forgiving. On another level, this inquiry is the beginning of a whole new relationship with the Divine, and the self, in a much larger context. Here the inner voice can more easily be found. Everyone has an inner voice giving them direction and assistance on how to be and grow. Some people never hear it. Others do, but do not listen, they ignore it. Opening a conscious conversation with that piece inside of you allows you to move more quickly along your path. The questions then transform into: "What is God, what am I really, what is my purpose here, what do I really want, and how do I do this thing called life?" We will go deeper into this soon, but first let's review what we have discussed so far. **(ex#6)**

THE PROCESS

PSYCHOLOGICAL SUMMARY

Where we get stuck!
1. We get stuck in the past and in the future, never in the present.
2. We cling to painful experiences of the past that we were never fully able to accept.
3. We tighten in fear, trying to avoid similar painful experiences in the future.

Who gets stuck!
1. We all get stuck but it is not the "I" that we are aware of now, but rather the child that "was."
2. Because it got stuck, the child remains, still struggling with the feelings of that early wound.

How we stay stuck!
1. We try to hide, ignore, deny, even kill the inner child because its struggle is too painful to even acknowledge.
2. We develop a personality designed to cover over and compensate for the lost child.

How we get unstuck!
1. We recognize and acknowledge that we are uncomfortable.
2. We allow ourselves to experience the feelings now that we were unable to allow before.
3. We accept the feelings as being part of us and that they are okay.

4. We acknowledge that as small children we made the only choice we could, but that now as adults we can make a different choice.
5. We release the feelings and cease clinging to them, they no longer hold power over us.

How we stay unstuck!
1. We don't. We don't give it our attention. We stay present for whatever experience is here for us now in this moment "Now," without fear or preconception.

What is stuck!
1. We are unable to move forward and grow because we are living in the past and its pain.
2. We are unable to be fully present because we are living in the future and our fear of it.
3. Our lives are run by the fearful child within.
4. As long as we remain stuck, our relationships with others are about invisible wounded children reacting to projections of each other, based on pain and fear. We never really know ourselves or the other we are with.
5. When we react to something someone else says or does it is never about them, it is always about us and our opinion of what they said or did, based on our past pain and our future fear.

THE PROCESS

Now that we are moving into the metaphysical/spiritual aspects of the process, let's ask that question again.

What is stuck?
1. The life force energy that wants to flow through us can't. We will not accept part of it, we resist.
2. A piece of our life force/our soul gets lost and left behind to keep alive the painful experience.
3. We miss most of what is here to be experienced in this moment because we are unconsciously trying to live out all the wounding experiences of our past. We are never fully here.

JEFF BOYER

PART FIVE

JEFF BOYER

THE PROCESS

THE OTHER SIDE

So this is where we shift gears. Until now we have been looking at the origin of our pain and how to change it mostly from a psychological perspective. This perspective is based on an agreed upon set of boundaries and assumptions. Those boundaries and assumptions describe what we might call the finite self. The finite self represents a limited physical being who is born, is affected by the physical world, reacts to that world in a limited way and then dies. That is it! Great things can be achieved but the being is still limited and any real power or influences are projected outward on others and onto some transcendent source. What holds this together is that most people buy into it either consciously or unconsciously. As I explained in the psychological summary, this amounts to several billion wounded children trying to justify the pain they perceive coming from the world around them. Thank heavens not everyone buys into this childish view of life anymore. All the great spiritual teachers of the past tried to tell us the truth about life and this world we live in, but we did not understand. We misinterpreted what they had to say and chose to either worship them or kill them. Neither of these were what they had in mind. We could not understand them then but more and more souls are beginning to now. The main ideas that they tried to communicate were that we are not limited physical beings at all. We are unlimited spiritual beings and we all originate from the same source. We are created in the image of our creator which means our true nature, when realized, is one that consciously creates every aspect of our reality. We are not limited to or by what we can perceive around us.

There is enough information out there now about these issues, from many different sources, that almost everyone has at least heard something about the existence of other states of consciousness or being. I am talking in a broad sense about everything from mystical spiritual experiences to channeling and multiple dimensions of existence, unexplained spontaneous healing, near death and out of body experiences. Movies, books, and games are all full of this stuff these days. Where did these ideas come from, and why are so many surfacing all at once now? Scientists are now starting to investigate some of these phenomena, like what happens to the brain when people are in deep meditation, prayer, or focusing on healing someone. A scientific study has now shown that giving an act of kindness, receiving an act of kindness, or observing an act of kindness **all** result in increased serotonin levels and boosted immune systems. You end up happier and healthier. Scientists have stumbled on other relevant evidence. They have theorized for a long time that we use only 5% of our brain. Why is that? Why would a limited world that many say is the survival of the fittest produce such a situation? Obviously the other 95% is being used but we just can't explain how yet. Here is a clue. Scientists have now concluded that only 5% of the matter, or stuff, in the universe is physical matter that we can see. They are calling the other 95% dark matter, because they don't know what it is even though it is most of existence from their point of view. Some versions of **String Theory** now postulate the existence of

THE PROCESS

multiple dimensions as a way of explaining dark matter. It just is not accessible from our current frame of reference.

Mystics and great spiritual teachers have known this for thousands of years and have had access to it because they do not limit their experience to what is understandable and explainable from just the "mind's" point of view. There is so much that is beyond the mind. What is ESP and how do we explain when people know something that is happening to someone else somewhere else? Why do we feel heavy or like the life is being sucked out of us when there is an angry person in the room, even before we know they are angry? Why do we feel better about ourselves when we are in the room with people who are at peace with themselves and their lives? Why are people flocking to alternative healing modalities, aura readings, hypnosis, past life regressions, psychics etc...? The answer to why all this is happening comes from within each person and at the same time from the same source. Let me explain by setting up some new parameters, or should I say lack there of, for the next part of our discussion. Try to set aside the ego and its judgments long enough to imagine what it would be like to live in this other reality, a spiritual reality that I am going to describe. This is the spiritual reality of Jesus, Buddha, and all the spiritual masters who ever walked the earth.

JEFF BOYER

SPIRITUAL REALITY

Stage one: Imagine for a moment that you are a being that was never born and will never die. You just are. You are immortal and eternal. Now imagine a Source, a Divine ... whatever, that you are a part of. You are not the whole thing, but part of the whole and have the blueprint for the whole inside you. As a part of this Source you have everything you need and have all the attributes of the Source. In fact, for the most part, you don't experience yourself as being separate or different from the Source at all. You are not physical, just consciousness, energy, light and vibration. The only thing that you or your Source long for is to experience more of what you are and could be, to expand into the limitless possibilities of knowing the self, and creating the self. This imagined being is what we might call the Infinite self, the Divine self, the Soul. Now lets set the stage for your physical birth.

Stage two: You become aware of this experiment called earth, where souls are going to experience what it is like to be physical and experience their Divine nature in a new way, thereby adding to the overall experience of the Source knowing itself. But there is a catch. In order for the self to experience the self as something, there has to be something that it is not. And since the Infinite self is part of everything that is the Source, there has to be some voluntary division of the self, so you can have something to compare yourself to. So you agree to temporarily forget where you came from and what you truly are. You set up goals for yourself in this new place (earth), and set about trying to gain broad experience, creating yourself as you go. Imagine now that many of you have been coming back here time and time again for more. "I

THE PROCESS

could have gotten more out of that lifetime, I would really like to experience being that kind of person, I want to go back and help others on their path more, I want to learn more about the experience of forgiveness." Some of you may have been going back life after life for thousands of years, but then something started to change. Your more recent lives where about beginning to remember what you really are and where you came from. You wanted to experience your full Divine nature while still in physical form, much like the spiritual masters of the past. You wanted to consciously create who you want to be in each moment.

So here you are today! What do we know about your life from this new perspective? First off, you have no finite self. The illusion of separation from your source is a creation of the mind, of fear, as I mentioned before. This was a useful tool which allowed you to be here and experience yourself as separate so you could then choose to be one again. ***Without the illusion of separation there could have been no choice and no real experience of the self, because the self is already one with everything.*** I know that part can be confusing so let me reword it this way. In the beginning you knew yourself to be everything, but could not experience it because there was nothing that you were not. You had nothing to compare yourself with, therefore no way to say I am this. When you say I am this it implies there is some other thing you are not. Got it?

So here you are and everything you experience is of your own creation or the joint creation of several souls, communities, or "humanity" as a whole. Events in the world at large are the result of the total collective consciousness, or unconsciousness, of humanity. The illusion of separateness from your source is followed by the illusion of need. Your body has needs but your soul does not. It had everything before entering this life and still has it now. The soul cannot be harmed in any way. It is immortal and eternal. Remember, you are not a physical being, but rather one of pure energy, spirit. Science is starting to back this up now with the study of quantum physics. The deeper we look into the physical, the less physical we find. At its core, matter is simply fluctuations in an energy field giving rise to subatomic particles, which temporarily relate to other particles, then disappear back into the quantum field of energy from which they came.

You are pure energy, and you create everything you experience. What you put your attention on is what you get in your life, because you, like your source are in a constant state of creating. Again, science has verified this in the laboratory where it was found that when observing subatomic particles, the experimenter's expectations affected what was seen. It depended on who was doing the looking and what they expected. So therefore you have everything you need and everything you expect in each and every moment. So before we go back and discuss your current life path from this perspective, we just need to address two small issues, *free will* **and** *destiny.*

Do human beings have free will or are their lives predestined? In the spiritual framework that we are looking at, the answer is ***both***. Everything is predestined, and everything is free will. "How can that be?" you say! Easy, you set it all up ahead of time and have the choice in each moment to

THE PROCESS

follow the plan or not. It is said that the soul can see the first thirteen years of life before entering the body. This means that you knew what the circumstances of your birth would be. You picked your parents, siblings, sex, race, socioeconomic class and the day and time of your birth to the second. The timing piece is your astrology which defines the starting position and initial set of qualities and challenges you chose. You are set to go but are free to change your mind in each and every moment of your conscious, or unconscious, life. You can either say yes, internally, and accept the experience in front of you, or you can say no, close down and contract in fear, which is what the infant did with its early wounding experiences. Let's try not to judge the choices as right or wrong, good or bad. Let's just say that they are different choices with different experiential outcomes. After all, if a soul really wants to experience the energy of forgiveness, it will need something that is difficult to forgive. Choosing not to forgive and living with that is just as much a learning as choosing to forgive what seems to be unforgivable. Maybe it means doing something to someone else and learning how to ask for forgiveness, forgive yourself, or learn how to feel worthy again to receive it. It is all learning and it is all creating as you go.

BACK TO THE BEGINNING

So now we can start back at the beginning with those perceived wounds we received as children. Having chosen a particular set of qualities and challenges to develop, the child responds to the wounding events in a way that will aid in the desired outcome. The thing to remember is that when you are born, you no longer have any memory of the plan and choices you made. Your soul knows, but not the child, the developing ego/personality. So you start to move through your early life collecting experiences, wounds, and building a personality, and some blockage to the flow of life energy that you are. You develop a set of beliefs to help you make sense out of the way the world works, but that does not change the fact that life hurts. The ego/personality believes that life hurts because someone else is to blame, or that the inner child is somehow to blame but does not know how or why. It, and the world, must somehow be deficient. If we take on a religious or spiritual belief, it is almost assuredly an externalized divinity, with transcendence placed outside, somewhere beyond the self. This serves to further dis-empower us, and God becomes another outside influence to be feared or blamed like a parent, a judgmental, needy, and insecure parent.

So the pattern was chosen, the wounds received, and the gifts start to be developed in the chosen areas where we wish to be of service to the world. The gift that the soul seeks to give is in the area of the wound. How else could it be? The gift may be for the learning experience of our own soul, for those we come in contact with, or even for the planet as a whole and its enlightenment. But in any case, we are "Stuck." The Divine light energy that we are is not flowing. We may

THE PROCESS

do wonderful things in the world to help others, but we are still in pain and often do what we do because it makes us feel temporarily better. We do it because it seems to relieve a sense of guilt or shame, or because we are actually afraid not to help others. Again let's not make judgments here for there is nothing wrong with helping others, unless they don't want our help. We do it for these emotionally charged reasons because we have not yet remembered who we are and what we are doing here.

Until we free up the life energy that is us, and moves through us, that which we can create remains limited. We remain limited because we believe we are limited. In truth, we are creating who we are in each and every moment, but most of us continue to do so unconsciously. We continue to create more of the things that seem painful, because that is where our attention is. We don't think that we are the ones in control of our pain, so we continue to experience our selves as victims of it. We remain ignorant of the creative power we wield. All thoughts, all words, and all actions are energies that create and attract more of the same. Think of the mind as a projector and your life as the movie screen. We are continually creating and projecting our own perceived reality on to the world around us. Until we finally begin to do so consciously rather than unconsciously, we remain victims of our self created ego/personalities and all their fears. We think those fears, we speak those fears, and we act out those fears, solidifying them in our reality. We then invest in what we have created by adding emotion to them. We take a thought, and connect it to a body feeling or reaction to create an emotion (energy in motion) for that thought. This is a powerful bond and when similar situations arise we immediately feel it in our body. We recoil from the feeling and often never even associate it with the original thought. We are "Stuck."

THE PROCESS

PART SIX

JEFF BOYER

THE PROCESS

GETTING UNSTUCK FROM THE OTHER SIDE

So now that we are looking at the metaphysical spirituality aspects of our perceived pain, how do we get unstuck? We have many more choices here, and they can work independently or in conjunction with each other and with our psychological work. The choices in this arena may sound easier but they involve willpower and discipline, acceptance and surrender. Like any change, it is a matter of your **attention** coupled with your **intention**. And here you thought maybe this side would be less scary than the psychological side. Not so! But it does get easier faster, once you get started. In my own life, it was the spiritual quest that came first, psychological quest followed, and later, a number of years where the emphasis went back and forth between the two. Now they feel like one and the same thing, just different views of the same life.

It could be said that the purpose of psychology is to heal the wounded ego, and the purpose of spiritual practice is to transcend or get rid of the ego. And, it would appear that these two goals are at odds with one another or at least that the healing of the ego needs to come first so that it can be offered up later. Not so, or at least that is not my experience. I don't see them as separate at all, but rather the same process occurring on different levels of the same consciousness simultaneously. They are both the process of releasing blocks to allow the life force energy of the individual to flow more freely. Trying to avoid future pain while still clinging to and identifying with the original pain is the blockage within the ego/personality. Mistakenly identifying the ego/personality as the true self is the blockage within the spiritual aspect of the individual. The ego/personality is a necessary piece of being human because it allows us to experience ourselves as individual, but it is just a small piece of who we really are. Likewise, there will always be some pain and fear in the human experience because it allows us to know, choose, and experience the opposite of pain and fear. So let's choose some tools now for getting unstuck.

TOOLS

The most logical place to start is with an approach that is respected in all spiritual traditions. In every religion, there is a deepening mystical level, where the wise and enlightened end up. Those are the one's that most of us have looked to for answers and inspiration at some point in our lives. These people, teachers, masters, or saints all have had one practice in common. They all took time for silence. Call it meditation, prayer or whatever, they spent time every day in silence, and here is why. That is where we most readily find God. That is where you can find the REAL you. In the silence, between the breaths, and between the thoughts is the resting place of the infinite self, the self that knows no separation from the Divine. There is only one thing that can keep you from reuniting with your Divine/Infinite self, and that is you. The little ego/personality "you" will bug you. It won't shut up, telling

THE PROCESS

you that "this silence stuff is for the birds, a waste of time, even bad for you." "There are so many other things you could and should be doing with your time." The basis of this distraction mode is the same as we discussed earlier, FEAR. The ego/personality is afraid of the silence and the dark, because that is where the pain is hiding, and if we sit too long and are too quiet the pain may come up. The ego/personality is all about protecting us from that pain, so it will get antsy and try, to distract us.

In order for this method of getting unstuck to work, you must choose to ignore the cries of the ego/personality and continue to refocus on the silence. This does not mean denying the feelings that come up, but rather, acknowledging them, releasing them, and then refocusing. There is no perfect way to do this! It is about the intention and the attention. If thoughts keep coming up, then watch the thoughts. As long as part of you is separate from them, watching them, then there is a part of you that is at peace. This supports the larger you. One great way to do this is to focus on the space between things or words. Pick a favorite poem or saying and start by focusing on one word at a time and then pause on the space between the words, between the thoughts. Just breath and relax into that space. Some people have trouble with focusing on nothing and so you can choose to focus on some thing instead. A traditional way to do this is to focus on the breath. Just breath in and out trying not to control or interfere with it in any way. Just watch it happen internally. Listen to and feel the breath but resist doing anything other than observe it. Try not to evaluate any part of it, just be the neutral observer. You can also choose to focus on things like a special word or phrase, a simple sound, or focus on an object or mandola. Any one thing can be an opening, a doorway to the soul, but no particular thing is required. The idea here is to focus on the one thing until you become one with the thing. Beyond that you and the thing may both fade away and you find yourself in a more expansive space, where you are the space, expanding outward without limits. Again there may be resistance and disbelief.

TRUST

Trust is the key. Trust your perceptions, don't judge them. Scientists studying the brain have now shown that the mind cannot tell the difference between what it sees in front of it and the memory of that thing. In addition the mind only perceives a small portion of the information coming in through the senses. It is selective. What it perceives is affected by what it believes is real and by what it expects to see based on past experience.

So it does not really matter if the perceptions make sense in your normal reality. There is no way to judge that your "normal" reality is valid except that maybe a majority of people in the world appear to live in it. So what! Look what they are doing to the earth and each other. We know now from our earlier discussion that most people are simply reacting to their environment out of fear, from the wounded child within. Do you really want to live your life based on that kind of normal?

In moving forward, discipline and willpower are required in order to ride the waves of resistance to the calm on

THE PROCESS

the other side of the river. Once you have identified that what you are includes that calm expansive space, then the psychological work is made far easier as well. It becomes easier because now a piece of your consciousness knows that the feelings of pain and fear will not be the literal death of you. You are, somehow, safe! You can then choose to experience, accept, integrate, and release those feelings of pain and fear from childhood, knowing that the larger you is standing by as a safeguard. It is protecting you from any real harm and is calling you through to the other side. The experience is one of being held up by the hands of God. You realize that the feelings are part of you, but only a tiny little part of you. In this place you can feel without being the feelings or being controlled by the feelings. You can acknowledge "the part" your personality plays and know that you are not your personality. This is the one essential truth that, if understood completely, can free you from nearly all the pain of life. When the realization comes that your finite self, your ego/personality, what you thought was you, is really just a tiny little piece of who you really are, you are free. You are free because you then have the choice to identify with the larger more infinite you. Of course this happens slowly over time as you learn to access those parts of yourself more easily. And the little you, the ego/personality will resist as it feels its influence slipping away. As its power over you does fade, so goes the fear and pain associated with it. **(ex#7)**

JEFF BOYER

CHOOSING

This brings me to a topic that may ruffle some feathers. Everything is a choice, and that includes feelings and emotions. When you break free from the control of the ego/personality, even for a brief time, you can begin to choose your feelings consciously. Sometimes it is necessary and appropriate to feel pain, and sometimes not. Let me explain. If someone close to you dies, if an important relationship ends, if you are witness to the suffering of someone you love, it is a natural response to feel pain. But feeling pain does not mean you have to become the pain and let it overwhelm you. When you allow it to do so it means you have touched into one of those areas I mentioned before where your own wounded inner child is hooked. I think it is also worth mentioning here something that Ekart Tolle talks about in his work. He calls it the "pain body". The pain body is a part of the ego/personality that identifies itself as the collection of painful experiences you have had. It feeds on pain because that substantiates its existence. But there is other pain that it carries besides your own personal pain, and that is collective pain, or the collective pain body. This can include the inherited pain of generations of dysfunctional family, the pain of a race, a sex, a nation, or of a religion. Triggers in the environment will give the ego/personality, the little "me", opportunities to feel and feed on pain. If the pain dose not appear, the little me will find a way to attract it, by provoking or triggering those around us to give us the pain it is seeking. Tolle promotes the practice of presence, or watching. When you watch the pain you are already separate from it to some degree. You are not the thought and the feeling but the one behind it who is having the thought and the feeling, therefor you are already separate from

THE PROCESS

the pain and can watch it. As long as you allow it to be and just watch it, it cannot sneak into your mind and take you over. You can also help others by being present for their pain and just holding a loving space for them and not reacting to *their* pain. This comes in very handy when they are trying to get you to react so they can feed on further experience of pain. Don't give it to them, just love them, even if they blow up and leave.

On the other hand, there are times when allowing yourself to go into the pain is desired. If you are in the midst of psychological work that involves your childhood pain, and that pain was never really accepted because it was too dangerous, then it will be helpful for you to go into that pain and identify with it in order to release it. If this is not the case, you have a choice. The more you practice the easier it will be to see the painful reaction coming and not identifying with it. When you begin to identify with the larger story of your Divine self then you can choose when to allow a particular emotion (energy in motion) to move through you. With the ability to choose comes inner peace. You can choose to be happy, even when from the ego/ personality's point of view there is nothing to be happy about. You can choose to allow the emotion of love to fill you and be expressed through you. Remember that the soul had it all before entering this life. It longs for nothing but to experience the further expansion of knowing its possibilities and adding to the experience of the Divine source itself.

When you can begin to entertain the possibility of living like this you will be amazed at the affect it has on your world. When you choose to walk around feeling the love of the Divine moving through you, it will affect everyone you come in contact with. People will be drawn to you. They will sense something special about you and feel better just by being around you. They will want some of what you have. Your life begins to move more smoothly, and you find yourself experiencing more of what is considered synchronicity. Things just start going your way, although it might not be the way you expected. People and circumstances just line up to present you with more of what you need. The people and opportunities were there all along but you where too busy, clinging to your old pain and trying to avoid new pain, to see them. Your life and what you wanted, at a soul level, was passing you by. **(ex#8)**

MORE TOOLS

So what other tools do we have in our spiritual tool box that can assist us in our quest. Oh, here is one. Ask for help! Sorry if you thought this one was going to be easy. I know it is really tough for a lot of people to ask for help. You are afraid of being turned down or rejected. You don't think that it or you are important enough. Some of you may even believe that it would mean that you were weak and needy. Well, asking for help can lead to a major shift in your life. Oh, I forgot, part of you is trying to avoid that. Anyway, when you reach out for help and say I can't do it alone, I need someone's help, the balance between fear and desire is tipped in the desire direction. It is pro-active rather than reactive. That is why it has been one of the cornerstones of the twelve step programs. When you reach out and risk experiencing

THE PROCESS

discomfort to get unstuck the universe rushes in to assist you.

So, who do you want to ask? Preferably someone who will listen and gently question without judging you. You don't need anyone telling you what you should or should not be doing. You want to pick someone you can respect and look up to because they have a quality you want. This could be paid help or a willing friend. If it is a friend, try to pick one that can be objective and not one that you are excessively emotionally involved with. Stay open, be real, and willing to risk those feelings that frighten you, and things will shift. Share where you are, where you came from, and where you want to go. Ask for feedback on any incongruence found between what you say you want and how you talk and act. Ask for reminders and to be called on the carpet for not following through. Ask them for support in experiencing your pain but not to let you wallow in it too long. Not only will you be moving forward, but you will not feel alone in your pain anymore. Someone who cares will be in there with you. It may be their uplifting energy, their presence, that inspires you to open up and allow the deeper you to surface, as you begin to feel safe.

There is another kind of help you can ask for as well. That help is from other dimensions, guides, angels, your higher self, God or whatever you want to call it. This kind of help can come in two different forms. The first is for understanding and the other is for direct assistance. The best way to ask for this kind of help is in a state of deep relaxation or meditation. Self hypnosis is a great tool and can be easily and quickly learned. The deeper you go the clearer the information will be and the harder it will be for the ego to deny it. Again, trusting yourself is the key. Try not to judge or discount anything you experience, just let it bubble up. It is often helpful to go on a little journey in your meditation. Go to a garden or place that is special in your mind, where you feel safe. Take in information from all your senses there, because it helps you go deeper. Wait for someone or something to greet you, ask questions and wait for the answers. The answers may come in words, pictures, feelings or just knowing. The latter is how I tend to get mine, I just get it, what they want to communicate.

If you want direct assistance from these guides or whatever you want to call them, it is important to think first about what and how to ask. Ask for assistance in what you are trying to accomplish within yourself, not for anyone or anything outside of you to change. Be clear and specific. Remember the law of attraction, because you attract what you put out. If you ask for the end of some difficult situation you give it your energy and attract more of the same. It is like telling the universe "this is the way I believe things are", and so the universe obliges you. If on the other hand you tell them that you are taking on certain new qualities and ask for their assistance they will come running to help. You might ask for help in becoming more open, kind, pro-active, peaceful, accepting of self and others. The list can go on and on. You can also ask for help letting go of certain things too, but remember to balance it out with a request for acquiring something positive in its place. That way you emphasize moving forward rather than trying to get away from something. Remember to always focus on a positive future. **(ex#9)**

THE PROCESS

POSITIVE THINKING

This brings me to one of the most powerful tools of all. I call it fake it till you make it. Actually, I am talking about projecting what you want and acting as if you already have it. The first time I ran across this idea was in Norman Vincent Peel's book on the power of positive thinking. I am sure it must have been talked about long before that and has been reiterated in numerous works since then, just dressed up differently. This is how it works. You concentrate on something you want to attain. Tell yourself that you can attain it, that you will attain it, that you are attaining it, that you have already attained it, and then allow yourself to feel grateful for already having attained it. From there on, act on that belief. Now you are creating that which you know already exists. So in our day to day lives this translates into "act happy and give thanks for being happy and eventually you will truly feel happy". Act as if you have let go of judgmental feelings toward others, and it will become your reality. This fits so well with the law of attraction that it is hard to tell where one stops and the other begins.

As I mentioned earlier, thoughts, words, and actions are all energy that you broadcast out into the world. If it is proactive caring sharing and accepting energy that you put out, then that is what starts to manifest all around you. If what you put out is reactive self focused and judgmental, then that is what you create around you. Note that this is contrary to the way things work in the business and political world. To a large degree, society has organized itself around the principle of the negative (read here: fear of lack, and of pain, me, me, me). It is about how to force things, that you don't want, to go away. It has not worked yet. There was even a war they called "the war to end all wars," but we keep having them. They may be smaller ones, but now we have more of them. The idea is that we pretend "they", the others, are different from "us" and judge them to be doing something we don't think is right, and then we decide that it is our right and obligation to make them stop it. This, all without ever asking them why they are doing what they are doing. We just shout out "stop it or else." And then we wonder why it never really fixes anything. This looks like a familiar parenting style, doesn't it? But if we bring it back down to the level of the individual, we find that this judgment of others as "less than" stems from an internal feeling of "less than." We don't feel good about ourselves and so we put others down in an attempt to lift us up. Believe me, it never works, it just keeps us stuck in our current experience of discomfort. At best, it allows us to temporarily cover over the experience of pain with a layer of anger. Either way, these behaviors are fear based, and in the end, our experience is still one of discomfort.

So how do you get started on this new pro-active lifestyle? Sometimes just listening to what comes out of your mouth for a while can be a good start. Notice if what you say is open, accepting, caring, and sharing. Or is it rigid, judgmental, reactive, and alienating? Later, if you can, begin to catch yourself in the midst of speaking in a non-productive way. Stop, change it, or say nothing. Move on, start trying to catch it in the thought process and change it there before you speak. What this comes down to, is imagining what the best and highest possibilities of YOU are, or might be, and then speak from that. Act from that, live from that, and most importantly project that. Remember, I am not saying that being reactive, judgmental, angry, and alienating is bad or wrong, so don't use it as another opportunity to judge yourself as not good enough. It is just another creative choice. Just know that when you are in that place, you have identified with an illusion. You are reacting based on the belief that you have lost something or are afraid of losing something that does not exist. It is a creation of the mind alone. When you become conscious again, and can see yourself in a more objective way, begin to identify with the larger you, the you that has nothing that can be lost, project that out into the world and see what *it* creates. **(ex#10)**

GETTING PRACTICAL

So lets get practical about this so that we can apply it to real life. Lets start with a simple situation and play this through. How about war, for example? Lets assume for a moment that you don't like war, that's not hard to imagine. Here is the change in energy that would have to occur in order to have a positive effect on your life and the world around you. Again, if you allow yourself to judge others as wrong or evil, focusing on your anger or fear, then that is what you give your energy to, and what you cultivate in your life. Protesting against war actually gives energy to the presence of war. On the other hand, holding peace vigils and getting together with people to envision how to create peace brings a whole different energy to bear. Imagine what a peaceful world would be like and then start acting that way to those you come in contact with. Create a peaceful neighborhood, city, and country, first, by being an emissary of peace. Modeling peace attracts more peaceful energy to you and affects those you meet in the same way. In politics, vote for the candidates that have ideas that are in harmony with yours, with what you want to create your world to be. Don't vote for someone because they are running against someone you dislike or worse yet, because you are afraid of what will happen if the other candidate wins. That is a choice that perpetuates fear. If you have noticed, the thing missing here is judgment, and in its place is discernment. Work toward what you want, what you would prefer, not against something you don't want, something you judge as wrong.

Out in the world, as in your own psyche, the only way to create positive change is not to struggle against what seems to be painful, but to acknowledge that the painful feelings are within, accept them, release them, and work toward what you want instead. Choosing to see life as a struggle is a choice. Choose again, choose differently. Be pro-active, not reactive. Remember that your energy affects those around you. When you shift from being contracted in fear to being expanded in love, you make more of that energy available to the world around you. Life is full of experiences and situations that can trigger you into being reactive. You may want to lash out or collapse inside. Know that there is a reason for that. If you "go off" on people, or if you collapse into depression, the result is the same. In an attempt to avoid feeling the discomfort of the situation you stay stuck and perpetuate that cycle. The more you struggle the more you stay stuck. If on the other hand, you see it happening and ask "What is it in my own psyche that is getting hooked?" then you actually have some control. Search inside! Drop down into the feeling and find out what needs to be accepted, and what needs to be released.

THE PROCESS

If we are talking about war, then there is something for most of us to get hooked by. The child within resonates with the victimization of innocents, the abuse of power by those who are stronger, or the fear of losing someone close to us. We may get hooked in a fearful way or an apparently hostile way, but it is still about the little child, our wounded inner child. Looking on the psychological side, we can take these reactions as a gift, a sign post of what needs to be looked at. From the metaphysical/spiritual perspective it is a call and a reminder to work towards staying in the moment, not fearing the future or clinging to the past, but breathing and moving forward in openness allowing yourself to feel as you go.

I am not saying that no one should fight against what they perceive as evil. I won't deny the existence of that reality for some. If that is what you believe to be real then that is what you need to do. But if you are reading this book and following what I have put forth, that is not for you. That is not your true reality. You can see beyond to the bigger picture. For the real change in this world comes from a shift in consciousness, which you can help with, not a shift in circumstances. When you are centered in the knowledge of being more than the circumstances of life, then it is possible to ask yourself in the midst of a perceived negative experience, "Who do I want to be in the face of this?" Ask yourself, "What is the highest possibility of me?" Then act from that place, that feeling, as best you can. This not only shifts your consciousness, but the consciousness of everyone around you and humanity as a whole. So what is the greater good, and how do you best assist that? Go inside and ask!

JEFF BOYER

GROUP ENERGY

Our discussion of community and the world at large leads me into the discussion about the combined energy fields of groups. One of the things that makes it so hard for us to change as individuals is the collective belief systems of those around us. The work place, the church, the neighborhood, all take on a collective energy and an accepted set of norms, including what is acceptable behavior, speech, and even thought. One way to shift the tide for yourself is to join or start groups that are open and progressive. This way you won't be struggling against the flow all the time. Groups of like minded people can raise the energy of all the members. Find a men's group, women's group, or a group based in meditation or other spiritual pursuits. Prayer circles, drumming circles, or any kind of open-minded, mutually supportive group will be a boost in your journey. If you can call a group of people together who all are willing to share their pain and their love, their struggle and their joy, and be present for each other, calling each other forward, then everyone's growth gets accelerated. This also gives you a grounding, a home base for your new energy that starts to flow. There is a comfort in difficult situations, when you remember where you are accepted as you are, for all of who you are. This mirrors the comfort found in dealing with your ego/personality issues when you remember you are more than the story, you are infinite and eternal.

THE PROCESS

THE LISTENING MODEL

If you are struggling with the idea of these tools, and nothing is clicking for you, and nothing feels right, here is one that takes no particular belief system to use: Listen! Just listen! When you are in conversation with someone, or in a group and you are made aware that the person who is speaking has a lot of emotion behind what they are saying, listen! Practice putting your own thoughts and feelings aside for a time. Don't judge what the person is saying, and don't think about how you feel about what they are saying, just listen. Try to really get what it is they are feeling behind the words. Then check it out. Reflect for that person. Give a summary of what you think you heard them say, and what you think they are feeling. Don't worry, they will let you know if you didn't get it, and they may then try to clarify their intended meaning. If you are right, they will let you know that as well, and may actually drop down to some deeper feeling, the issue under the issue. This is because when they feel heard, they feel safe and valued. Again, listen to that new expression, until they get to the bottom and it feels like they are through. Check it out and make sure they are done.

Listening is a form of practicing presence. If you are unable to accept your own stuff, your own feelings and what is happening in your life and be present for that, then you can begin by being present for someone else. Psychologists, counselors, and good friends do it all the time. Their own lives may be a mess, and they can't deal with it at all, but they often are perfectly present for others. For them it is natural because helping others is a priority. It is either part of their job or they are emotionally involved and capable. In either case it takes them out of their own stuff, their own feelings and pain, and gives them something to focus on. They feel better for being able to do it. They are helping someone every time they do it, and at the same time they unconsciously step into a larger part of themselves by detaching from the incessant noise of the little ego "me" in the head. Now to take this to its completion one can, after practicing on others, start to be present for oneself. You can refer back to the sections on meditation and positive thinking for a refresher.

THE PROCESS

JEFF BOYER

THE PROCESS

PART SEVEN

JEFF BOYER

THE PROCESS

GOING FORWARD

This brings us back to the struggle between the infinite self and the finite self, the higher self and the ego/personality. This essential struggle is the only REAL struggle that exists. All else is the creation of the mind. Even this is a creation of the mind seeking to maintain control and fearing annihilation. The ego/personality seeks to maintain its beliefs and opinions about what it has experienced and so becomes the source of all new pain. So how do we do something about this pain? Again, we shift our attention and our intention. We stop feeding the will of the ego which is all about "I want, I need", and begin nurturing the will of the higher self, which is all about "I am". In that place you find that loving yourself sometimes means denying your wants on the ego level and choosing something else. It means disciplining your actions, your words and even your thoughts. It means holding the knowing that you are more than your feelings, more than your body, more than your mind. It means focusing on what you want your life to become and at the same time knowing that you are already perfect the way you are. It means trying to see the best in yourself and the best in other people, to the best of your ability. **(ex#11)**

JEFF BOYER

STAYING PRESENT

So how do we guard against getting stuck in the future? We don't! We don't give it our energy. What we do is enjoy being in the moment. When something feels uncomfortable we listen because it is a signal that we are resisting, something that longs to be accepted or released. We take the feeling in and accept that it arises from there. We allow it and know that it is okay, without judging it, ourselves, or anyone else. If action is needed, we take it. We then release the feeling and return to being present for what is, here in this moment, now, without preconceptions. We are in the NOW, creating who we are and who we want to be, in this moment.

Remember, this journey is a gradual one, although sometimes it will feel slow and other times it will fly. Know that the times that it flew were when you were in the moment, allowing what you experienced to be as it is. You were happy, laughing, focused, inspired and engaged. You will probably rise to these heights and fall, over and over again, on your way. Know that it is okay and that it is all part of the PROCESS. A process that was meant to be experienced and enjoyed, not feared. Have fun and see life as a game to be played for the fun of it. Remember, you are immortal and eternal. Have fun and help others have fun. By this I mean, help others to see the potential in themselves by valuing them and pointing out what is enjoyable about them. Help them to laugh and to get out of the seriousness of "my pain", "my drama". Listen, share, and will them well. Model what you learn along the way and people will be drawn to you.

THE PROCESS
ALL ONE THING

So, to pull this all together I have to say it is all about one thing! Psychology, biology, astrology, cosmology, spirituality, religion, physics and metaphysics, sociology, numerology and on and on are all about the same thing. They are the mind's attempts to understand and make sense of existence from its own limited perspective. These things cannot be fully understood with the mind or by the mind. They can only be experienced. Experienced by the mind yes, but also by the emotions, by the body, and by something beyond that, something more than that. Life is energy in motion. Pain comes when we resist or cling. It is funny now to think of those old jokes talking about "life is like a river". But there is some truth to that saying. Life is beautiful when we watch it flowing by, or when we get in and go with the flow. If on the other hand we try to dam it up to hold onto some experience we had, or to try to hold off some experience from happening, we experience the pain we seek to avoid. We stop flowing, we are stuck. This is the area that both psychology and metaphysical-spirituality attempt to address. The healing that is sought in both these arenas is the same thing, the un-damming of the river. They both attempt to remove the blocks where we got stuck.

In both cases it is, in effect, the releasing of old belief structure. In the psychological realm, the beliefs are centered around concepts of the personal self. In the realm of spirituality, the beliefs are around our infinite nature and our perceived separation from our source. They are not on a continuum, one following the other, but rather different layers of the same thing, the same being. They flow in the same direction at the same time in the same space.

Again, each person's life and experience of it is different, yet not so different. We all experience pain, and we all seek to be free of it. At the core, we all want to love and be loved unconditionally. We want to be accepted as we are. We want to feel like we belong, really belong. Those who have experienced God, or source, will tell you that was their experience. They felt loved and accepted just as they are. They finally felt like they were home where they belonged. What I have been trying to explain in this book is actually the Process of learning to treat yourself the way God, or source, or whatever you want to call it, would treat you. It is about opening up and allowing the love, the light, the energy that our source offers us. It is about manifesting that light and love in us, and then radiating it outward to all that is. You see, there was never anything wrong in the first place, you just thought there was. It is so hard to see when you are caught up in the drama of it all, it's true. It has all been our choice and our creation. All these things, situations, fears, are all for the purpose of opening us up to the experience of Divine love, and to know it for the first time from a feeling state. In our broken-ness is the seed of our true wholeness, our oneness. When we crack open and grow, we get to experience more of what life and love could be. It is only by first having the experience of not being divine that we have the choice to experience ourselves as divine, and choose to own that truth.

Now, here at the end, the purpose of this book has become clear to me. It is about helping those who are ready

THE PROCESS

to change, see that the pain they have experienced is a gift. It is a gift in that it provides both the motivation to change, and the keys, the doorways to that change. If it were not for our pain, we would never change and grow. Without pain, there would be nothing with which to compare the experience of love, peace, joy, and ecstacy. How could we ever really experience being alive, and know the true meaning of that if first we had not experienced the feeling of being dead, stuck, and unworthy, fearful, angry, and hurt? What I hope I have conveyed here is that if you can open up to see the bigger context, the eternal you, and see your experiences of life as self created or co-created, then everyone and everything in your life, starting with the pain, becomes a doorway to the possibility of joy and union with your God, your source. This is where my path has brought me and has compelled me to share it with all who will listen. Thank you for honoring me by reading this book. Thank you for honoring yourself by trying on the feelings it awakens in you all.

My thoughts and prayers go with you all,

Jeffrey Thomas Boyer

JEFF BOYER

WORK BOOK

Ex#1 Your Story

1. Make a list of memories starting with the earliest ones.

2. List the key events and changes in your life, the pivotal moments.

3. Write a brief story of your life using parts one and two. Include other information such as details about the family members you grew up with.
> Example: My father was angry a lot of the time when I was growing up, and he was seldom home. My earliest memories of him were when he was yelling at me or telling me that what I was doing was wrong. Later after my parents divorced he tried to be my buddy, the one or two times a year when I saw him. My mother...........

Ex#2 Your Gifts

1. Make a list of your gifts. These are your talents, skills and special abilities. Don't be shy, include every little thing you do well, especially those things that end up helping other people or the world at large. Be generous to yourself here. Even singing in the choir is a gift. Being able to truly listen to

THE PROCESS

people without interjecting what you think is an enormous gift to those people because they feel valued. Are you a deep spiritual thinker? Are you creative in some way? Are you a leader, an organizer, or mediator? Maybe you are just good at loving people! Maybe you are really good at your job. Make it a big list!

Ex#3 Your Fears and Aversions

1. List your fears, all of them. If you are afraid to make this list for fear someone will find it and use it against you, write that down too.

2. List the things you can't stand, can't tolerate in yourself as well as others. What makes you really mad? What really frustrates you? What makes you painfully sad?

3. Read over these two lists and look for patterns and similarities. This means getting general, so be specific about it.
>Example: I can see from my lists that I get triggered by people who act in ways that seem disrespectful of others. Most of the people I get angry about are those who I think have power over me........... It looks like what I fear most is other people's judgments........

JEFF BOYER

Ex#4 Looking at a Different Past

1. Looking back at your list of memories and the short story you wrote, think now of a different way your life could be described. If someone else had all the facts and pieces what other kind of story or stories could they make up?
2. Write a very brief description of your life as a hero, one as a victim, and one as a comedy. Find the details in your life that can support these views. It doesn't have to be a big production, a few paragraphs will do. If it feels good and you want to write more, write more.

Ex#5 Solo Work (trying it on)

1. First you need a place where you feel safe and will not be interrupted, a place and time where you don't have to worry about noise and who might hear you. This may take some planning, or on the other hand, it could take some letting go of what others think of you. Just tell them "I had to work some stuff out."

2. The only equipment you need is something soft to lay on like a mattress and some darkness or a makeshift blindfold. Sometimes background music can help, but it needs to be something without words, and preferably not too familiar to you.

3. Being scared is perfectly fine and appropriate, but if you don't have a sense that you will be okay, no matter what happens, then stop here and work on the other exercises. If

THE PROCESS

having someone else present who you trust would help you feel safer, do that.

4. Get started by reviewing your story, your fears, and your aversions. Lay down on your back and close your eyes or cover them as mentioned. Relax and let everything just swirl around without focusing on any one thing. Begin deep breathing, and gradually increase the speed until you begin to feel a little light-headed. Don't worry! If you pass out you are already lying down and your body will take over regulating your oxygen intake for you. When you reach this point, see if there is a sound that will come up. Try making a sound, a grunt, a growl, a scream. You will know it is right if the sound wants to get bigger. It may feel like you are struggling not to make a sound, that also means it wants to get bigger and it wants to get out. Just let it happen and let it out. Go for it! If the sound becomes yelling at someone about something, especially if it is in your childhood, stay with that. Play it out. You may be experiencing yourself as a child, or as your adult self trying to protect the child. Continue the conversation, and if you can, start speaking both parts. Be the person you are angry with and speak for them too. Be all the parts of the conversation. Notice the opportunities that arise to make different choices than were made when you were a child. When the energy dies down, think about whether or not the scenario has been played out to the end. Did you create some closure for yourself? Did you make choices? How do you feel about it? If nothing comes after the sound, just a release, know that "that" is what you needed, and enjoy the lightness that follows. It may be that nothing happens in language, and your body just wants to move or shake or vibrate. If no sound or movement comes, just swirl around in your images and

breath until one thing seems to grab you. Talk to it. Ask it what it has to teach you. Try some role play with the different characters in a given memory. Find their motivations and see if it gives you some understanding. You may feel spent afterwards, especially if you did a lot of yelling. Make space for yourself to just "be" for awhile. Remember that choosing to look at this stuff at all, is both courageous and an act of conscious self-creation.

5. Whatever happens, write it down before you forget it all. Make note especially of those things that surprised you or had lots of energy in them. Also, write down those areas where you felt you could not go or were too scary. Consider dialoging with them or ask questions about them in one of the following meditations.

Ex#6 Inner Guidance

1. What most of us don't realize, is that we are being talked to all the time we are awake! When a situation arises and you have an immediate positive response or knowing of what you need to do, that is your inner voice. We just don't listen to it very often. We push it away because it does not necessarily match our emotional reaction. The longer we think, the more reasons we find not to act on that first inner knowing. We don't trust it.

THE PROCESS

2. (Journey Meditation.)
One of the best ways to deal with this is to consciously choose that guidance, consciously ask for it. Find a quite place and sit upright with your head supported and begin to follow your breathing. Close your eyes and allow yourself to become more relaxed with each breath you take. Slowly count your way down from five to one, and with each count, let yourself drop down deeper and deeper into relaxation, more comfortable, melting into the chair. Give yourself a bit of time to get as relaxed as you can allow. Then, imagine you are walking along a path somewhere in nature, a path that leads to a garden, your garden, your special place where you feel totally at peace. Imagine there is a gate and you enter, close the gate behind you and find that you are safe and completely at peace. Walk in the garden paying close attention to what everything looks like, sounds like, and even feels like. Walk around noticing your surroundings until someone or something friendly comes to greet you. Know that this is one of your guides for the moment and part of your inner voice. It may be someone you knew who died, some spiritual figure, an animal, an angel etc. It doesn't matter what form it takes. Greet this presence and ask it if it has any information that you should be made aware of. Trust what you get! The information will be imparted to you in some way that you can receive it. It could be in words, sounds, images, feeling, or just an internal knowing. The form does not matter, just trust what you get. Trust it because it comes from a deeper part of you. Thank your guide, leave the garden, and close the gate. Count yourself up again from one to five slowly, becoming more awake and alert with each count. Then, return to present time and space. Take time to write down everything that you remember about your garden and your meeting. If you just

can't seem to come up with any information just enjoy the deep relaxation and take another journey to the garden in a day or two and see if the information starts becoming clear for you. Don't give up! Your inner voice and higher self are always trying to speak to you, keep listening for it.

Ex#7 "The Larger You" (a meditation)

1. Find a comfortable place to sit with your feet flat on the ground and your head supported. Close your eyes and begin to notice the places in your body where you are holding tension or are feeling uncomfortable. Touch, rub, shake, or stretch those places. Don't try to get rid of them necessarily, just give them a little bit of attention and then let them go and drop down into your breathing. Deeper and deeper you go with each breath, more and more comfortable, more and more relaxed, feeling yourself melt away into the chair, the air, the earth. Begin to count yourself down from five to one, and with each count find yourself becoming more and more comfortable, more and more relaxed. Now imagine you are walking along a path, seeing, hearing, smelling and sensing everything that is going on around you. Ahead there is a place, a special place just for you, waiting for your arrival. It is a comfortable, safe, and relaxing place, and you settle in, ready for what is going to happen next. Imagine a movie screen appearing in front of you. On the screen is playing a movie that you have seen before. As you watch you begin to realize that it is the movie of your life, and you are just watching it play. You are relaxed, sitting back, just watching it all go by. You are enjoying the show, the whole thing up there on the screen. You stay focused on your breath to let

THE PROCESS

yourself know that you are *watching* the movie, separate from it, not in it. You may have feelings about what you are seeing, but you are not attached to those feelings. In the next moment that scene is gone, and another one takes its place, playing itself out before you. "Interesting", you think! You notice more about the movie this time because you are not caught up by it. You watch, and at the same time, stay centered on your breath. Now go deeper into the breath. Just watch the breath, don't try to do anything. Be the breath. Just be. As you relax into being, notice that the screen seems to be getting smaller. Then, you realize that it is actually you getting bigger, expanding. You become lighter and gently expand outward. You realize that the movie screen is now only part of you, a small part. You encompass the screen and the special place where you were. You encompass the ground and the air around that place as you breath. You become lighter and larger. You begin to pay special attention to the spaces between the breaths, the silent, seemingly empty spaces between things. Rest there. Rest in those spaces. And as you rest in those spaces, become aware that those spaces make up most of what is, seen and unseen, heard and unheard, felt and unfelt. Breathe into those spaces and let those spaces breathe into you. You are now in all things, and all things are in you. You are as old as the beginning of time, immortal, eternal, omnipresent. Enjoy that feeling for awhile. Then when you are ready, start to bring yourself back to that special place. Smile at the screen and know that the story is but a small piece of who you are. You are larger than that. You are the breath, and you are the spaces between the breaths. Take a breath now and know how big you really are. (Continued in ex#8)

(Optional ending): Allow yourself to be in that space for a moment and when you are ready, begin to bring your awareness back into your special place. Put the screen away for now and know that you can return here any time you wish. Begin to count yourself back from one up to five, becoming more awake and alert with each count. Find your way back to your path and then slowly bring yourself back into this time and space, bringing all the memories and feelings of the experience with you. Write down or record everything you can remember.

Ex#8 "Create it Different"

1. Imagine the movie playing again and you begin to feel that you know what is coming next. Decide now to make it different. Make this next clip, this next scene, go the way you want it to. Create it now. While you are creating, keep in mind this larger *you* that you now know exists. Remember that this larger *you* already has everything it needs because everything already exists inside it, and so needs nothing in particular. What do you want to create? How do you want to be in the presence of what you see happening on the screen next? What part do you want to play, what role? Pause and take a deep breath. Ask the bigger *you*, what am I here for, what is my purpose? The first thing that comes up is probably the key to it. Trust it no matter how grandiose it may seem. Then when it starts to become clear, create the next scene with your purpose mind. Watch it unfold before you and let yourself fill with gratitude for having the opportunity to create it. Let the feelings of love and gratitude wash over you as you watch your newly created story unfold, and at the same time

THE PROCESS

be aware of how you are still connected to all things through your breath. Let the joy of knowing and the joy of being, fill you up and spill over the top. Notice the joy coming from everywhere around you as it fills you and moves through you and out again through your breath to the world. Let the knowing sink in now that all of it is a choice in each moment. Resolve now to choose consciously, purposefully. Choose with joy and love and deep peace as your guides. Be in that peace for a moment before returning to your special place and know that you can feel this again, any time you wish. Let all you have learned sink deep into your bones, your very cells, and take it with you. Choose to remember it all. Put the screen away and begin your journey back. Begin to count yourself up from one to five, feeling more awake and alert with each count. Slowly return to your path and to this time and place, retaining your resolve to create your life with your new understanding.

2. Jot down any key memories, changes and decisions that you made. Write down any "aha's" or major feelings.

Ex#9 Asking For Help

1. Find a comfortable place to sit with your feet on the ground and your head supported. Follow your breathing down. Count yourself down from five to one. Become more comfortable with each and every breath, more relaxed and more peaceful. Find your way now to your special place. Many people find this to be a beautiful garden with a gate, a place made just for them alone. But, it can be any place, real or made up, where you feel safe and supported in your journey. Drop down into

your breathing now, not trying to do or change anything. Just watching the breath, becoming the breath. When you are completely relaxed, look around your special place and take in all the details you can. Notice what everything looks like, smells like, and feels like. Find a place there to rest and wait. Just being present to the place.

2. Now imagine that someone or something is coming to greet you. This will be your teacher or guide for the moment. Notice everything about them. This being has been waiting for your arrival and has lots to offer and share with you. Greet them now and receive a special gift that they have brought for you. Thank them and hold your gift, letting its significance sink into your being. After you have looked your gift over, ask your guide a specific question about something that is going on with you that you feel you need help with. Wait for the answer to come to you. This information could come as words, feelings, symbols, or a simple knowing. Ask for as much clarification as you need or just know that if it is not clear now, that it will become clear when the time is right. Now your guide has a specific piece of information that they want you to have. Wait and receive it as before. Thank them for helping you and say goodby till next time. Go over what has been shared with you, the gift, the answer to your questions and the message they had for you. Tell yourself that you will remember all of it as you return to your awareness of your special place. Look around again and then make your way back to your path and count your way back up from one to five and become fully awake and alert in this time and place.

    (Don't forget to write it down!)

THE PROCESS

Ex#10 Further Assistance

1. Repeat the previous exercise and ask not only your guide but any and all other beings who are present to assist you, including whatever name you use for that Divine source that you came from. Ask them to be with you and to help you achieve your goals of self change.

2. Examples of things to ask for:
Help me to release all negative thinking, and to accept the love and support that is available to me all the time.
Help me to accept myself and others without judgment.
Help me to see that all things are complete and whole and perfect as they are.
When things feel like they are getting difficult, help me to step forward and act, not step back and react. Help me to always be pro-active.
Help me to be more caring, and sharing, and helpful because it makes everyone feel better when I do. And it makes me feel more fulfilled.
Help me to open up and receive the gifts that spirit has to give me.
Help me to see how I create my reality and help me to choose it consciously.

Ex#11 Positive Thinking

1. Get into a relaxed or meditative space.

2. From what you have learned about yourself so far, focus on something that you have not yet manifested in your life that would be beneficial to your growth and happiness. It could be

something you have been longing for or something you just recently realized is part of your purpose and destiny.

3. Examples of positive thinking:
(Define the desire and then follow these steps.)
A. I want to develop the ability to speak in front of large groups comfortably. I can learn how to speak in front of large groups comfortably. I will learn how. I am learning how. I have learned how. Then go deep into the feeling of being able to speak comfortably in front of those groups. Visualize or imagine yourself in front of a group now. Let yourself relax as you imagine the scene, with you comfortably speaking. Let that feeling wash over you, "I am doing it and it is easy and natural to me." Next, go into the feeling of gratitude for having learned how to do this. Let the feeling of gratitude overwhelm you. Repeat this process daily for several weeks and at the same time, take the steps you know were needed for you to accomplish this task. For some people, that would look like planning a series of times when you would speak in front of groups and run through the positive thinking process just prior to each time, visualizing the whole thing happening and how comfortable you are with it. For other people, this might look like signing up for a public speaking class where everyone has the same goal. Again, run through the process prior to each class, focusing on the feeling of comfort while speaking.

B. I want to be more successful at my job. Go through the steps; I can, I will, I am. See yourself doing it, let yourself experience the feeling of being more successful at your job. Go into the gratitude of having achieved it and let that feeling fill and overwhelm you. During this process you might even

THE PROCESS

learn what steps or actions a more successful "you" took to get there. Act on those. If not, run through the process daily before work and then notice if what you are doing or how you are doing it are consistent with a more successful "you". Remember to first run through what you know about yourself so far, looking for those things that would be of benefit to your growth as a person. So, if you become more successful at your job, don't be surprised if you get a raise, a promotion, or get fired. It may mean that you need to move on to something more important or fulfilling and satisfying.

Ex#12 Moving Forward

1. Discipline! One of the most important keys to moving forward is discipline. The ego/personality is used to running the show. "I want, I need, give me that, I'm scared, I can't, I won't, etc. It sounds very much like a small child if you think about it.
Start with something you can stick with, and stick with it. Know that anytime you say I am going to do this or that and then don't follow through, your little ego/personality says "See, I told you that you couldn't, wouldn't do it." "That proves that you are no good, unworthy, weak........" So once you decide, stick with it no matter what. No Matter What!
NO MATTER WHAT!!! This is how control is shifted away from the ego and towards the higher self. It does not even have to be something that makes sense. In fact it is often better to pick something that makes no sense because that eliminates many excuses that you can come up with not to do it. Example: Decide that you are going to go outside at five AM sharp every day for seven days and through a ball up in

the air and catch it 120 times. Come rain or shine, wind or snow, follow throw. Let your ego know that what you say you are going to do is exactly what you are going to do. Just keep throwing the ball up and each time it comes down say "thank you". The ego is going to whine and complain, and you just tell it to shut up. Let it know that you have already made up your mind.

Once you have begun to establish some control, start to pick disciplines that will be beneficial to your personal and spiritual growth. Yoga, meditation and regular exercise are highly beneficial, as is dietary discipline, but no particular thing is required.

2. Be impeccable with your word! If you say you are going to do something, do it. If you're not sure, don't say anything, or say maybe, I'll have to see. Be sure what you say is true for you. Never say something just because it is what you think someone else wants to hear. Don't repeat things that others have said as if you believe them, unless you really do. Stay within what is true for you.

3. Reserve judgment! This does not mean that you will not make judgments, rather it is a decision to set aside judgment for a time. When others are speaking, just be totally present for them. This shows respect and concern for others and will help you understand them and yourself. As you practice not speaking or interrupting others, you will be presented with a variety of your own feelings, insecurities, and tendencies that you will learn from. Don't judge these internal responses as bad. Just be present for them. Then ask yourself, "isn't that interesting?" Then return your attention to the speaker and what is being communicated.

THE PROCESS

4. Don't expect others to be conscious! Even though you may be becoming conscious of what you think and say and do, don't expect others to be able to do the same. Stay with what you have control over, and that is you and only you. Remember to be a role model, not a fixer. There is nothing wrong with anyone anyway. Stay inside what you know to be true from your higher, more infinite self.

5. Consciously choose how you do what you are doing! Whatever it is that you have decided to do, whether it is the kind of work you do, or the dinner you are putting together, the group you are meeting with or the exercise program you are involved in, choose to do it in a way, and with a consciousness that benefits the highest possibility of you. Ask yourself, "Who do I want to be, and what do I want to create, in the presence of what I am experiencing now?"

6. Review what happened! Begin a practice of reviewing your day before sleep, and think about how you employed these consciousness keys throughout the day. When you feel that you have used them to the highest good of self and all, rejoice in what you have created. If on the other hand, you find situations where you could have benefitted from being more conscious, don't use it as an opportunity to judge yourself as "less than". Instead, just notice and resolve that in similar situations you will try to be more aware of what is happening and what you are creating. Practice observing yourself and choose from that place.

7. Take care of yourself! This means doing the things you know are good for you and following through with them. Again don't start if you aren't going to follow through because

it sends the ego the wrong message. Eat what is healthy for you and only eat what you need not what you want. Get exercise and move you body to free up energies that might get stuck. Have fun regularly, laugh and dance and sing. Do things that help you get out of your head and stop thinking judgmental thoughts about yourself and others.

Note: Please feel free to adapt these exercises and meditations as you see fit. Repeat as often as you need to shift your thinking and feeling. Remember, this is all about conscious self-creation, so have fun creating yourself anew.

POSTSCRIPT

Here I wanted to talk a bit about what's beyond the Process, or maybe what should be called the process beyond the process. What are we doing this for anyway? I have talked a lot about pain and fear and the process really beginning when they become intolerable and you decide you have to do something about it, no matter what. But, most of the people in the world don't ever reach that point. They go on denying or ignoring their pain, taking it as just the way it is. So what is different about you that drives you to seek change? What difference does it make and what do you get when it's over, that most of the people in the world won't have a chance to experience.

It is about purpose. The whole thing is about purpose from before day one to beyond the last day. I am not talking about getting good at the right job or finding the right mate. It is much bigger than that. The purpose I am talking about is your soul's purpose, the reasons you came here in the first place. If you have gotten this far and are reading this postscript, it is likely that you are one of those who has chosen to be here for a high purpose. I am talking about a purpose that involves helping a great number of other souls on their path. It is about taking part in what many would now call the evolutionary shift of the planet, a global raising of consciousness. This is about not only consciously creating your own life the way you want it, but also about creating the planet of peace and love that every soul longs for.

So how does all of this tie in? First many of you but not all chose childhoods with what seems like an extraordinary amount of pain. Many of you ended up after childhood really feeling like victims, powerless and defective or insufficient in some major way. You may have had major abandonment issues feeling like you could never make it on your own. Through this kind of suffering you developed a great deal of sympathy and empathy for all those in the world who suffer. The reason for this was so you could consciously choose to create yourself to be the opposite. You gave yourself the opportunity and the motivation to become one of few who can literally change the world. Your ultimate intention, in spite of not believing it yet, is to become powerful, confident, and competent emissaries of your source. If you follow this process through to its natural conclusion, you will end up feeling like everything is perfect including you. To a large degree, you will feel complete within yourself. You will feel whole on your own and yet not separate at all, but rather connected to the whole the way you started out before fear found its way in after birth. So it is about coming full circle, returning to your source, but not by dying this time. This time it is about manifesting your true nature to the best of your ability while still here.

Obviously everyone's purpose and manifestation will be a bit different. But I do want to share with you some of the things that will be the same for all of you if you continue to open to your, what I will call, path of destiny. First of all you will notice that there is little or nothing in this life to be

THE PROCESS

frightened of. You will begin to understand the feelings and motivations of many of the people you see, even if you don't know who they are. Beyond that, you will actually feel love for those people without any reason other than you happen to see them or even hear them nearby. You will begin to experience the world as synchronous and meaningful in every way. I am not just talking about occasional coincidences either. I mean that you will start to see how most of what happens during your day is there to bring you to an awareness of your true nature, your Divine nature, which is connected to all things, is affected by and in turn affects all things.

As I spoke about in the book, being in the NOW is a process of its own. It means being aware of what is happening and allowing the feelings that arise to be. When you don't fight them or cling to them, but instead feel and watch them at the same time, their significance can be realized. Once the feelings and their significance have been received, the future and range of possibilities and probabilities one faces have already been altered in a significant and positive way. So what does that really mean? It means that by being fully aware of what is being presented to you, and not judging or trying to alter it, it leads to an opening in your life that could be described as flow. Each day and the things in it are there to open you to the experience of pure love and absolute connectedness. You are connected to your source and always have been. Your perceptions of victim-hood, pain, and suffering never changed that, they only made it impossible to experience.

What would it be like to live your life as the source of that life. What would it be like to walk through your day loving everyone you saw as if they were your own child, seeing them as perfect and beautiful as every newborn baby truly is. What would it be like to walk through nature and feel that its beauty is actually an extension of your own body, your own heart beat and breath and feelings. What would it be like to wake up each morning and know that you are perfect and you are in the perfect place having the perfect experience that is leading back to your source? Let's find out! Let's keep going! I have experienced most of these at times, some more than others, but the ride is amazing and getting better every day. Come on! Ride along with me! Let's change the world together!

The bumper stickers that I have on my car really say it all. **One: Don't believe everything you think!** The mind is a trap designed to keep you unconscious to your true identity. Don't believe it. Go past it to the quiet space of the void and find out who you really are. **Two: Something wonderful is about to happen.** Expect the next thing that happens to be exactly the perfect thing for you. Allow it and then let its meaning be revealed. **Three: There is no way to Peace, Peace IS the way.** Project what you want to see out in the world. Find the peace within you and let it out for all to see. You will be amazed at the results, time after time. It has been a true pleasure writing this book. It started out as an attempt to put on paper what I knew about life and how it works. I never imagined it would eventually end up writing itself through me, using me like I use pen and paper. These words wanted to find a way to get on paper and out into the world and it has been an honor to be the one who was called on to do it.